IMAGES
of America

RHODODENDRON

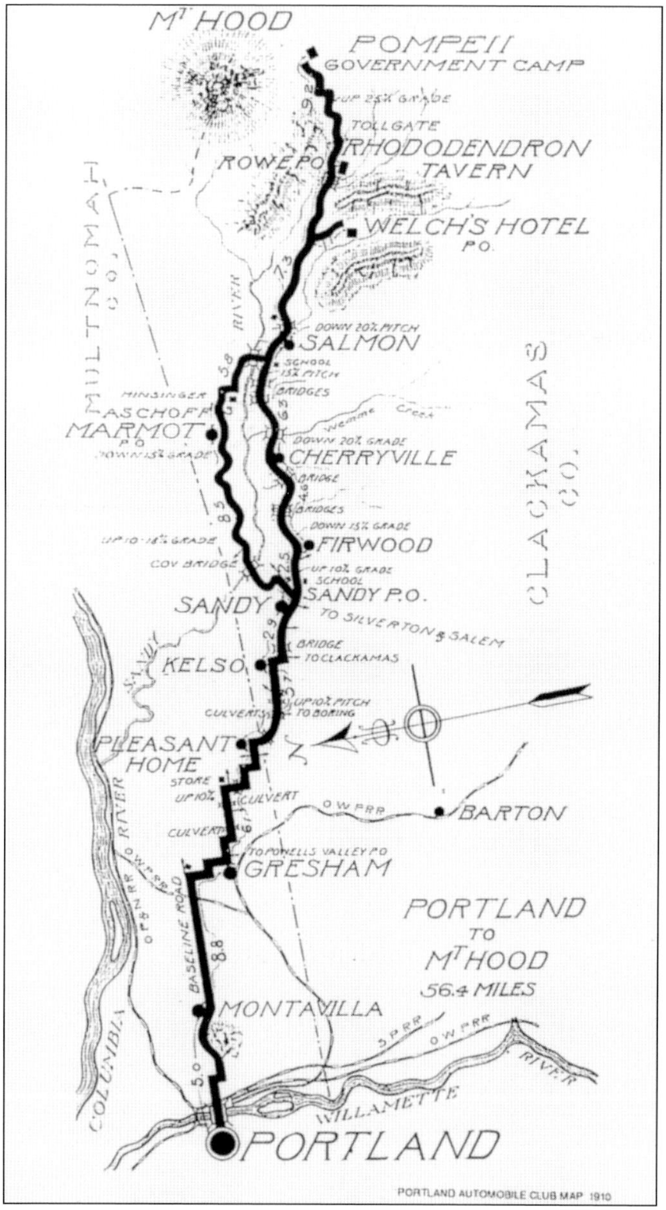

This 1910 Portland Automobile Club map shows the route between Portland and Government Camp, also referred to on the map as Pompeii. Getting to Rhododendron in those days was often a two-day trip. The roads were challenging, and travelers would often take frequent breaks from the rough ride and spend the night in Sandy, Cherryville, or any one of the small communities along the way. (Courtesy of Mount Hood Cultural Center and Museum.)

On the Cover: This photograph of the Rhododendron Inn was taken just after its opening in 1909. The inn was an opulent destination for travelers as they made their way up the Mount Hood Highway. Owned by former Portland mayor Henry Rowe, the construction of the inn started in 1907 and was completed in 1909. It was sited along the north bank of the Zigzag River, just east of the bridge where the Mount Hood Highway crossed over the Zigzag River into Rhododendron. Sadly, the inn burned to the ground in 1949. (Courtesy of Mount Hood Cultural Center and Museum.)

IMAGES
of America

RHODODENDRON

Steve and Judi Graeper

ARCADIA
PUBLISHING

ISBN 978-1-4671-0683-2

Published by Arcadia Publishing
Charleston, South Carolina

Printed in the United States of America

Library of Congress Control Number: 2021934591

For all general information, please contact Arcadia Publishing:
Telephone 843-853-2070
Fax 843-853-0044
E-mail sales@arcadiapublishing.com
For customer service and orders:
Toll-Free 1-888-313-2665

Visit us on the Internet at www.arcadiapublishing.com

Thank you to those who came before us, the indigenous people who would seasonally visit and set up camps along the rivers and in the fields of Mount Hood's western foothills. (Courtesy of Mount Hood Cultural Center and Museum.)

Contents

Acknowledgments 6

Introduction 7

1. Early Settlers 9

2. Early Rhododendron 21

3. Businesses 37

4 Movers, Shakers, and Other Characters of Rhododendron 69

5. Camps, Cabins, and Cottages 89

6. Nature's Wrath 113

7. But Wait . . . There's More 123

Acknowledgments

The gathering of information and photographs for this book would not have been possible without the support, advice, and contributions from the following: Lloyd Musser, Mount Hood Cultural Center and Museum curator; Gary Randall, photographer/historian; Ken Funk, director of genealogy/research, Sandy Historical Society & Museum; and Bill White. Thank you for answering our calls and emails whenever we had questions. Our appreciation and heartfelt thanks are also extended to the numerous individuals who contributed their family photographs and historical recollections. There are far too many of you to name individually here, but you are recognized with each picture that we have used.

Additionally, our sincerest appreciation and gratitude are extended to our dear friends Leslie Phillips, who spent countless hours and responded to numerous emails helping us edit our captions, and to retired English teacher Mary Carol Day, who graciously broke out her red pen and taught us a few things about punctuation and grammar. We could not have done this without you both.

Unless otherwise noted, all images in this book appear courtesy of Mount Hood Cultural Center and Museum (MHCC&M), Sandy Historical Society & Museum (SHS), and Oregon Historical Society (OHS). The authors of this book have agreed that all of their royalties earned on book sales will be donated to the Rhododendron Community Planning Organization.

Introduction

In the early 1800s, as word got out that great economic and social opportunities awaited those who dared make the journey out West, many early pioneers set forth looking for a better life. Scouting the way, they often followed existing trails initially established by the indigenous people of the area. Eventually, they blazed new routes to accommodate their trains of wagons as they embarked on the long and perilous westward journey to rich possibilities, including those of the Oregon Territory.

As more and more pioneers braved the treacherous routes West, the trails became rutted by hundreds of wagon wheels. Soon, names would be given to these trails: the Mormon Trail, the Bozeman Trail, the Santa Fe Trail, the California Trail, and the well-traveled Oregon Trail.

From Independence, Missouri, to the rich valleys of Oregon, the Oregon Trail brought many daring pioneers over the hazardous, nearly 2,000-mile-long route. Once the wagon trains reached the Wascopum Mission (now known as The Dalles, Oregon), they were faced with the expensive task of disassembling their wagons and rafting down the treacherous Columbia River. As they braved the river, many would be lost to the dangerous rapids at Celilo Falls, never making it to their final destination.

Then along came Sam Barlow. Barlow believed that "God never made a mountain that he didn't make a way to get over it." In 1845, Barlow and a scouting crew forged south and west from The Dalles and found a route over the Cascade Range along the south side of Mount Hood, sometimes following trails used by the indigenous people for hunting and gathering foods and medicinal herbs. In 1846, Barlow and Phillip Foster were granted permission to build a toll road that would be less expensive and less treacherous than the Columbia River route. Even so, the Barlow route was the most harrowing 100 miles of the entire Oregon Trail.

The Barlow Road opened in 1846. The direction of travel was effectively one way until 1861, when a better road was blasted through Laurel Hill. For the first few decades, emigrants followed the road seeking the land of plenty in the Willamette Valley. Once over the Cascade Range and just past Barlow's last tollgate, weary travelers could rest in the large meadows and flat areas to gear up for the last leg of their journey.

As more and more settlers established homesteads in the Willamette Valley, the lands in the Cascade foothills became more attractive. These foothills were rich in forested vegetation, flowing streams, and abundant wildlife. Settlements started sprouting along the Barlow Road.

On May 20, 1862, Ernest D. Sievers took up squatter's rights on 160 acres at a site just west of Tollgate No. 5, the last of Barlow's tollgates. This wide spot along the road eventually became Rhododendron, Oregon.

Rhododendron is nestled among the foothills of a sleeping volcano in a valley between Zigzag Mountain and Hunchback Mountain, where the geology is diverse, beautiful, and mysterious. For eons, the landscape has been sculpted by the eruptive activity of Mount Hood. Named for British admiral Samuel Hood in 1792, the majestic mountain was also known by some indigenous people as Wy'east.

The lush landscape of streams, rivers, forests, and glens created by Mount Hood has, for generations, attracted visitors to the area. Once discovered, pioneers, homesteaders, business entrepreneurs, and vacationers started the rapid transformation that shaped Rhododendron.

However, living in the mountains is not without some peril. Heavy snowfall, winds, and torrential flood-producing rains are common occurrences as the jet stream weather pattern shifts the clouds up and over the Cascade Range. Rhododendron and the surrounding areas have experienced many natural disasters. Historic floods were recorded in 1931, 1964, and 2011. Severe wind events like the Labor Day 2020 and January 2021 storms laid old-growth trees down like matchsticks, leaving devastation in their path.

Fire is another disaster that looms over the residents of Rhododendron. Fortunately, since the early development of Rhododendron, the area has not been too adversely affected by naturally occurring or human-caused forest fires. However, geologists and foresters agree that fires have and will continue to occur. The Burnt Lake Fire in 1904, which was started by a slash burn on the edge of Enola Hill, and the Mirror Lake Fire in 1931 are proof that the Rhododendron area is not exempt from dangerous fires. Had it not been for the favorable east winds that kept the 2020 Riverside Fire burning west and away from Mount Hood, the entire area could have been devastated.

In spite of the potential dangers, by 1907, the area around Sievers's original staked land claim became popular with valley settlers. Visitors were lured to the area by the lush green forest, the soothing sound of abundantly flowing rivers, and the comforting feel and smell of the crisp mountain air. With the Homestead Act of 1862 and, later, the US Forest Service establishing tracts for recreational cabins, visitors made the sometimes-two-day journey up the mountain on the Barlow Road. First on horseback, then in carriages, and then by primitive automobiles, the population of Rhododendron began to grow along with the supporting infrastructure. The US Postal Service established Rhododendron's identity, the Rhododendron Inn provided early shelter, and soon grocery stores, restaurants, service stations, and other supporting businesses followed. These businesses sustained the ever-increasing population of movers, shakers, and characters that was made up of permanent residents, summer cabin owners, and vacationing visitors. While some businesses survived, others faltered, which made room for new businesses to step into their place. Camps, cabins, and cottages were built, lived in, and enjoyed until suddenly being removed by disastrous floods. But floods, fires, wind, and snowstorms are pervasive in the mountain climate, and people adapt. Like their pioneering predecessors, the folks living in Rhododendron and the surrounding Hoodland area are resilient and strong. These people make up a caring and passionate community that steps in to help when neighbors are in need.

There were many more businesses in Rhododendron than are described in this book. There were many more movers, shakers, and characters than those profiled in this book. There were many more camps, cabins, and cottages than those cataloged in this book. But, hopefully, the essence, the heartbeat, and the willpower that were and are Rhododendron were captured.

Rhododendron is currently in a transitional phase. From the bustling community enjoyed from the 1920s through the 1960s, the attraction to Rhododendron has declined as the populace has followed growth into other nearby communities. The seductive call of the mountain still exists, and most have strong feelings as to how they react to that call. Some are called to bask quietly in the forested solitude. Others tolerate Rhododendron as just another wide spot in the road as skiers and valley vacationers rapidly whisk by on their way through the once-thriving community to the promising recreational slopes of Mount Hood. Still others recall the close-knit neighborhood that Rhododendron once enjoyed and are called to aid in a planned and much needed rebirth. This vision includes a community that promises to have safe access to businesses, safe crossings of a busy US Highway 26 for pedestrians, and a renewed beautification of the area to be enjoyed for generations to come.

On January 26, 2020, Rhododendron celebrated 100 years as a community. With input from caring citizens sharing ideas, dreams, hopes, and desires, perhaps Rhododendron can prosper for another 100 years. This book chronicles the history of Rhododendron, but the future of Rhododendron has yet to be written.

One

EARLY SETTLERS

Samuel Kimbrough Barlow was a pioneer road builder. In 1845, he joined the Oregon migration, leaving Illinois with his wife, Suzannah Lee, and their four children. When they reached the Wascopum Mission (later renamed The Dalles) near the Columbia River, it was the end of the wagon road. Travelers then needed to disassemble their wagons and raft down the treacherous river. It was expensive, and many rafts never made it through the very dangerous Celilo Falls. Barlow was determined to find an easier route. He believed that "God never made a mountain that he didn't make a way to get over it." In October 1845, Barlow led a scouting party with 19 other adults who blazed a trail across the Cascade Range around the south side of Mount Hood. Ten weeks later, on Christmas Day, after an arduous journey that necessitated leaving their wagons behind, they reached Oregon City. The following year, Barlow and Phillip Foster obtained a charter for the development of an 80-mile toll route that became known as the Barlow Road. Almost immediately, the Barlow Road became the preferred route to the Willamette Valley, becoming a toll road in 1848. (Courtesy of OHS.)

In 1846, Sam Barlow and Phillip Foster blazed an alternate route for the Oregon Trail across the Cascades. Although still treacherous, it was less so than rafting the rapids down the Columbia River. Beginning at the Wascopum Mission (now The Dalles), the Barlow Trail wound its way through the Tygh Valley and across the southern shoulder of Mount Hood and west into Oregon City. Barlow and Foster built a single tollgate to help defray the cost of building and maintaining the trail, and over the years, the tollgate was placed in five different locations to prevent travelers from bypassing to avoid paying the toll. In this photograph, taken sometime in the late 1880s, a freighter with a team of three horses pauses at Tollgate No. 5, the last of the Barlow Road tollgates. Barlow selected this site as it was difficult for travelers to bypass, being bound on one side by the Zigzag River and on the other by the steep mountainside of Enola Hill. (Courtesy of Bill White.)

Tollgate No. 5 was the last location for the Barlow Road tollgate. It was placed just east of Rhododendron and operated between 1879 and 1915. This 1885 photograph shows, at left, Ernest Sievers with his oxen team. Sievers was the first settler to claim rights in the Rhododendron area. Behind Sievers on their horse-drawn wagon are Sam and Sarah Bacon, and standing next to the horse team is Adam Kotzman, who lived at Bull Run. An unidentified herb collector is on horseback. (Courtesy of MHCC&M.)

Each tollgate consisted of outbuildings to house the gatekeeper and family, along with a gated wooden fence that would be opened by the gatekeeper after travelers paid the required toll. This photograph shows one of the early tollgates along the route. John Maronay served as gatekeeper here, and besides collecting tolls, he also maintained a trading post. (Courtesy of MHCC&M.)

Over the years, there were five different locations for the tollgate. This was the last one, Tollgate No. 5. Amanda and John Maronay were the gatekeepers for several years. The term *tollgate* meant just that: there was an actual gate in the fence across the road. The gate would remain closed until the travelers paid the toll, and then the gatekeeper would allow wagons and livestock to pass. The tolls at one point were $5 for each wagon and 10¢ per head for livestock. (Courtesy of Gary Randall.)

This group of young men in 1907 is standing at the Barlow Trail Tollgate, located a mile east of Rhododendron. From left to right, they are Gustave Stucki, Lloyd Baker, Harry Thornton, an unidentified male, John Maronay, and Arlie Mitchell. With pistols, rifles, and bottles in hand, perhaps they are getting ready for an afternoon of target shooting. (Courtesy of SHS.)

Arlie Mitchell, climbing on Tollgate No. 5, was the last gatekeeper, serving from 1905 until 1908, when tolls were eliminated. This was the final tollgate on the journey west. Located one mile east of Rhododendron, a replica of the tollgate still exists near the Tollgate Campground. Two big leaf maple trees were planted near the gate by Daniel Parker, a previous gatekeeper, during his employment from 1883 to 1889. They are listed as Oregon State Heritage Trees. (Courtesy of MHCC&M.)

With his steam-powered Stanhope, Dr. John B. Kelly drove the first automobile up the Barlow Road from Portland to his family's lot in Government Camp. From there, he drove three to four miles into the snowfields just above the timberline to load up 50 pounds of snow to take back to Portland. He is shown here crossing the Zigzag River near Rhododendron. He received a certificate from the tollgate keeper confirming the feat. (Courtesy of MHCC&M.)

Farming was difficult around Rhododendron because of the mountainous terrain, but grazing livestock was a common occurrence. In the above photograph, a herd of sheep that likely belonged to ranchers in the Shaniko area of Wasco County is being herded from the summer range in central Oregon, over the mountain, to the livestock market headquarters in Troutdale, Oregon. Each herd had a shepherd who would move the sheep to grassy areas along the way. Sheepherders had to have permits for grazing in the national forest while making the trip to the market. In the photograph below, a shepherd is driving his herd across the Zigzag River Bridge. (Both, courtesy of MHCC&M.)

Many of the early pioneers who traveled the Barlow Trail took advantage of the Homestead Act of 1862. Two of these early settlers in Rhododendron were William H. and Cynthia Creighton. They homesteaded a parcel of land located just east of Rhododendron at the 2,800-foot level of Enola Hill. (Courtesy of MHCC&M.)

William and Cynthia Creighton, who homesteaded on Enola Hill, are pictured here. They were known in the area for this horse-drawn buggy. (Courtesy of MHCC&M.)

Here, Cynthia Creighton is drawing water from the well. Her son Walter wanted her to move down from Enola Hill to his property in Zigzag. He built her a house on his land with the hope that as she got older, she would eventually move in with him and his wife, Elsie. Being very stubborn, Cynthia did not want to move. One day when Cynthia went to town with Elsie, Walter took all of her belongings out of her house and burned it down, thereby forcing her to live with them. (Courtesy of MHCC&M.)

James Walter Creighton was the son of William and Cynthia Creighton, born on November 6, 1877. Known as Walter to his friends and family, he was a man of many skills and interests. He and his wife, Elsie, claimed a homestead near Rhododendron in 1905 and built a small two-room cabin. Walter was a fine carpenter and built many homes and barns in the area. He and Elsie were well known and became pillars in the community. In addition to being a fine carpenter, Walter was also a freighter. With his heavy wagons and fine horses, Creighton would haul large loads from Portland to central Oregon by way of the Barlow Road. Walter Creighton died on his homestead at age 88 in 1966. (Both, courtesy of MHCC&M.)

This is Elsie Creighton on her dapple-gray horse around 1925. In 1905, Walter and Elsie Creighton claimed some of the last land available for homesteading in the Rhododendron area. Elsie served as the secretary of the Welches School for decades. She had an interest in local history, and both the Oregon and Clackamas County Historical Societies came to Elsie for historical knowledge and artifacts. (Courtesy of MHCC&M.)

The Homestead Act of 1862 provided homestead ownership of land. To qualify, settlers needed to build a dwelling and work the land by raising crops or livestock. Ernest D. Sievers, a squatter, had chosen this land because it was flat and had nice streams as well as a large open meadow that provided hay for wagon teams as they traveled the toll road. In 1903, Heinrich Haman bought the homestead rights and gained ownership to the 160 acres. Haman then built this homestead cabin on the property. The cabin remains today, but it has been updated several times. (Courtesy of the Lamoreaux family.)

Two

Early Rhododendron

This is the main street of early Sandy, Oregon, with majestic Mount Hood in the background. People traveled through this little town on their way to Rhododendron and Mount Hood. The dirt roads were rough and rutted. Often, in low and swampy areas, a corduroy road would be made by laying logs side-by-side perpendicular to the direction of the road. The journey from Portland to Rhododendron would sometimes take two or three days. (Courtesy of Gary Randall.)

Rhododendron was a stop on the way to Mount Hood for stages that transported guests up the old road in horse-drawn carriages like this one. Many people wanted to reach Government Camp to meet up with a guide who would take them climbing to the top of Mount Hood. (Courtesy of Gary Randall.)

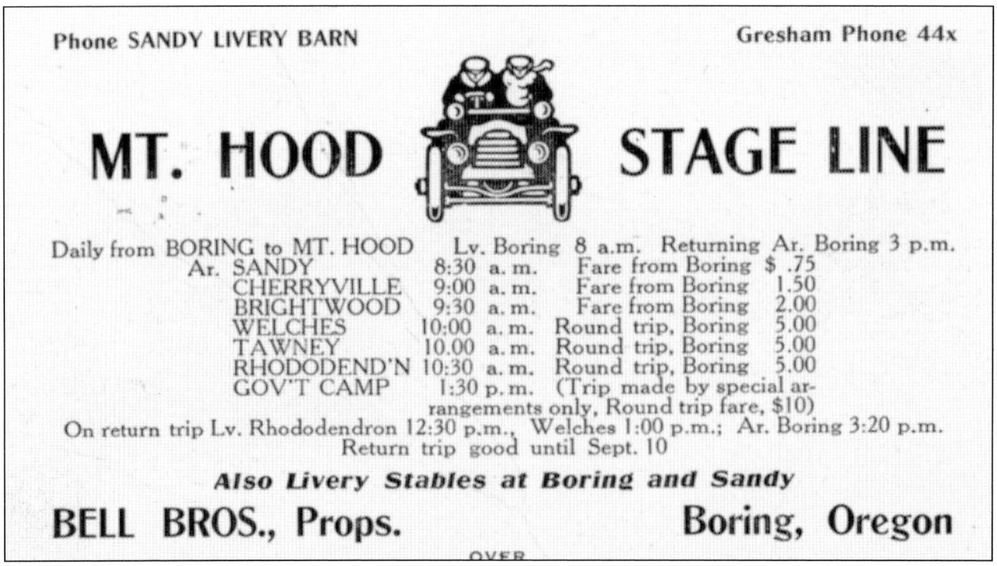

The trip to Mount Hood by horse-drawn carriage sometimes took several days. The automobile was the answer to the lengthy trip. By 1914, motorized stage service companies that provided access to Mount Hood were in full swing. This is a rate card for the Mount Hood Stage Line. It shows the rates for various destinations along the route from Boring, Oregon, to Government Camp. (Courtesy of MHCC&M.)

This log gateway along the Mount Hood Highway was located near what are now Lolo Pass and Faubion Roads. In 1920, it marked the entrance to the Oregon National Forest. Seen here is photographer Fred Donnerberg, who was on his way to check the progress of the road to Lost Lake. The Oregon National Forest would later become the Mount Hood National Forest. (Courtesy of Gary Randall.)

In the foreground is the Mount Hood National Forest marker at the corner of East Lolo Pass Road and what is now US Highway 26. Still in its original location, it continues to mark the western boundary of the Mount Hood National Forest. In the background is the Gateway. Built in 1916 by the Bear Creek Land Company, it served as a café, filling station, store, hotel, and post office. It was renamed the Zigzag Mountain Store in the 1970s and was condemned as unsafe in 2005. The building was extensively restored in 2008 and currently serves as a restaurant. (Courtesy of Gary Randall.)

Travelers Roost, later known as the Zigzag Inn, was built between 1927 and 1930 by William Lenz. Working sometimes with the help of his son William "Bill" Lenz, he built many log structures in the area, including the Mazama Lodge, the Barlow Trail Inn, and cabins in Mountain Air Park. He also built the Log Lodge in Rhododendron. Lenz was a natural mathematician, and despite a lack of formal training, he drew beautiful blueprints. Whenever he was commissioned to build a house, he would draw up the plans, fell the timber, hand hew the logs, and build the structure with precision craftsmanship. He also built artisan custom furniture. (Courtesy of Stephen Kenney.)

Henry Spoor Rowe and his wife, Agnes, moved to Portland, Oregon, in 1880. He worked for the Oregon Railroad & Navigation Company and then in banking until serving as mayor of Portland, Oregon, from 1900 to 1902. After his term as mayor, he returned to his work in the railroad, banking, and real estate industries. In 1907, Rowe and former Portland fire chief Lee G. Holden purchased 160 acres from Heinrich Haman and began building the Rhododendron Tavern, later known as the Rhododendron Inn. Sited along the north bank of the Zigzag River, just east of the highway where it crossed the Zigzag River Bridge, the inn was an opulent destination for visitors as they traveled the Mount Hood Highway. After construction was completed in 1909, the US Postal Service established the Rowe Post Office, with Lee Holden serving as the first postmaster. Rowe passed away on March 20, 1914. (Courtesy of OHS.)

This is a photograph of the Rhododendron Inn taken sometime in the 1920s. In front of the inn is a Reliance Stages vehicle used to transport visitors from Portland to Rhododendron. In 1912, Emil and Susette Franzetti, European hoteliers, bought the Rhododendron Inn. They transformed it into a bustling European-style resort serving fine cuisine. The inn was built in 1909 and burned to the ground in 1949. (Courtesy of Gary Randall.)

After the Franzettis purchased the Rhododendron Inn and surrounding 150 acres, they eventually added a dance hall, a swimming pool, tennis courts, bridle paths, hiking trails, and an annex across the highway. In 1916, after Emil Franzetti was killed in a rollover automobile accident, Susette Franzetti subdivided some of the property and began selling buildable lots. She contracted with Henry Steiner, a log cabin builder, to construct cabins on her lots. (Courtesy of OHS.)

At the Rhododendron Inn, guests could enjoy learning how to weave and spin yarn. This corner was especially popular with those who did not particularly enjoy outdoor activities. To spend the night at the inn cost $4 per day or $18–$21 per week, with special rates offered for families. (Courtesy of Gary Randall.)

Here, one sees a cozy corner of the lobby at the Rhododendron Inn. Guests took advantage of the airy bedrooms, great halls, comfortable porches, and relaxing living room. On cool evenings, guests were known to gather near the great fireplace to share events of the day. (Courtesy of Gary Randall.)

Emil Franzetti was a trained European chef, having served in many fine restaurants. He stated in a brochure he penned about the Rhododendron Inn that one of his greatest honors was preparing a meal for His Majesty the King of Italy. To Emil Franzetti, preparing fine food was an art. On the grounds of the Rhododendron Inn was a large garden used for growing vegetables. In spring and summer, the fresh, succulent, homegrown vegetables were incorporated into the fine meals he would serve. In addition, the Franzettis raised chickens, which provided eggs and meat for recipes, as well as Jersey cows, which provided fresh milk and cream for coffee and making butter. (Courtesy of Steven Kenney.)

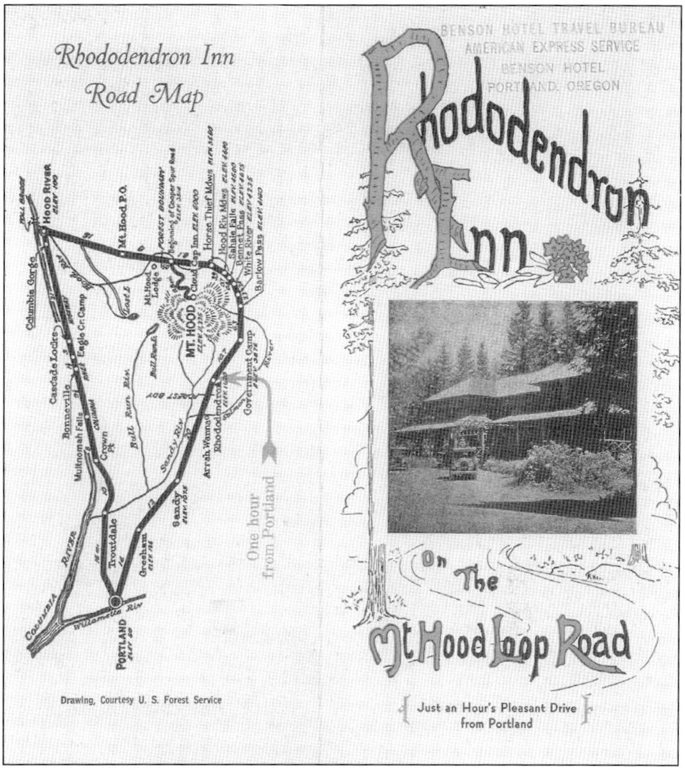

Widowed after her husband, Emil, died in an automobile accident, Susette Franzetti ran the inn by herself for seven years. In 1924, she sold the Rhododendron Inn to William Cash. He produced this brochure of the inn that was made available across the Portland area. In 1948, Cash sold the inn to Thomas Rex, who renamed it the Rex Inn. On February 2, 1949, the Rex Inn burned to the ground, touched off by a blowtorch that was thawing frozen water pipes. (Both, courtesy of Gary Randall.)

The Ideal Vacation

combines diversion with rest, invigoration with relaxation, good food attractively served, with beauty of surroundings, and all at moderate cost.

Rhododendron Inn

offers this, with the additional advantage of being within one hour of Portland, while yet buried in the heart of mountain and forest.

The atmosphere of complete remoteness and seclusion, so prized by vacationists, is here, notwithstanding direct telephone service and the ready access to one of America's finest highways.

Our Hobby

You will enjoy our hobby of weaving.

Flax is one of Oregon's coming products and is receiving a great deal of attention from the public. We have on display many interesting articles made from the excellent products of Oregon linen mills. These were hand-woven by us, and make useful and beautiful gifts.

We have an old loom and spinning wheel in a corner of the lobby where we weave and spin Oregon wool.

We will be pleased to have you stop to see this interesting work.

Sport for All

Each season has its own attraction: fishing, hunting, hiking, skiing and snow-shoeing parties gather here, and leave a trail of happy remembrances.

One of the most popular sports is horseback riding along the charming bridle paths that follow the ravines for miles.

Where Appetites Are Reclaimed

No greater tonic is needed than fresh, clean mountain air and pure, cold spring water.

Special pride is taken in the preparation and serving of food.

The huge fire place in either end of the spacious lounge makes the Inn a fine place for special dinner and dancing parties.

Rates Are Moderate

$3.50 up per day, single, American Plan
$6.00 up per day, double, American Plan
Special weekly and monthly rates

Dining Room Service:

Breakfast	$ .50	Dinner	$1.00
Luncheon	.75	Sunday Dinner	1.25

Address, mail or phone
Mr. or Mrs. W. F. Cash, Operating Owners
RHODODENDRON, OREGON

In 1910, Dr. Dav Raffety discovered a mineral spring near the Rhododendron Tavern on property he purchased from Henry Rowe. He dubbed it "The Fountain of Youth" because of its exhilarating effect. In 1911, Henry Rowe, Lee Holden, and A.T. Lewis started the Rhododendron Mineral Springs Land Company. It was a real estate development company that specialized in hotel and summer resorts and was responsible for laying the first water lines to serve the community. In this photograph, a couple is resting on the logs covering where the spring comes above ground. (Courtesy of Gary Randall.)

After purchasing the Rhododendron Inn, the Franzettis added an annex across the highway from the main building with eight more rooms, another kitchen, and a sizable dining room. Several more cabins and tent sites were also added to accommodate more guests. Unfortunately, the annex was consumed by fire in 1932. (Courtesy of Gary Randall.)

Summer recreation was a draw for many prominent Portlanders. They would come to the Rhododendron Inn to rest and to enjoy the great outdoors. There was much to do when visiting Rhododendron, including fishing, hunting, hiking, swimming, and playing croquet or tennis. The tennis courts, pictured here, were very popular. (Courtesy of Gary Randall.)

As part of the expansion of the Rhododendron Inn, a swimming pool was constructed by Emil and Susette Franzetti. The pool is estimated to have been built in 1915 and was across the highway from the inn. It was referred to as the "swimming tank," and the water was heated by the sun. (Courtesy of Gary Randall.)

The original Rowe Post Office was established on February 23, 1909. It was located in Dad Miller's Grocery Store just west of the Rhododendron Inn. Lee Holden was appointed the first postmaster. From 1909 to 1920, the area around Dad Miller's store and the Rhododendron Inn was known as Rowe, Oregon, in honor of former Portland mayor Henry S. Rowe, who built the Rhododendron Inn. The Rowe Post Office served the area from 1909 until 1917. On February 27, 1917, the Rowe Post Office was decommissioned by the US Postal Service. The post office was moved down the road and renamed the Zigzag Post Office. On January 26, 1920, the US Postal Service commissioned a new post office near the Rhododendron Inn and named it the Rhododendron Post Office because of the abundance of native rhododendrons in the area. From then on, the town of Rowe was known as Rhododendron, Oregon. (Both, courtesy of Gary Randall.)

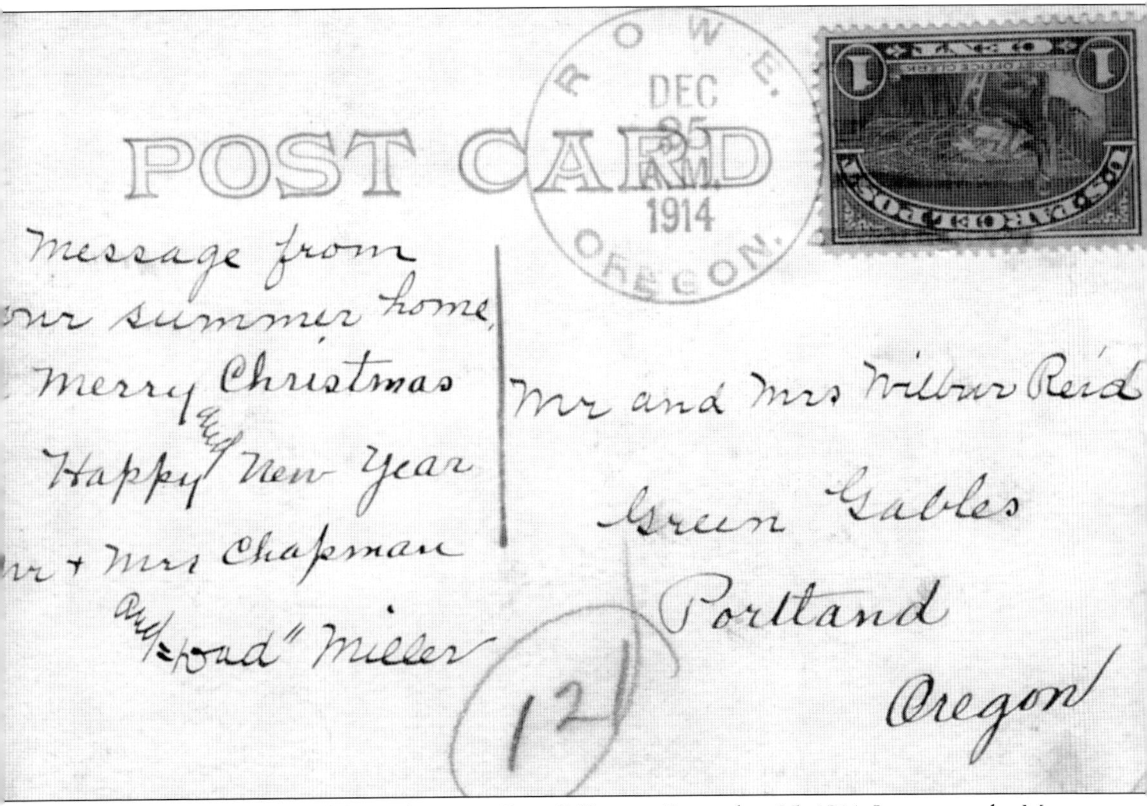

This postcard was mailed from the Rowe Post Office on December 25, 1914. It was sent by Mr. and Mrs. Chapman and "Dad" Miller to Mr. and Mrs. Wilbur Reid. The Reids' cabin, Alderbrook Lodge, was the first summer home built in Rowe, Oregon. The card reads, "A Message from your summer home. A Merry Christmas and Happy New Year." (Courtesy of the Reid family.)

Cynthia Creighton is seen here standing on the porch of the Rhododendron Store. The store was likely built around 1920 in the town that had recently become recognized by the postal service as Rhododendron, Oregon. Better known to everyone as Ma Creighton, she and her husband, William, had a homestead on Enola Hill just east of Rhododendron. (Courtesy of Tom Anderson.)

This Rhododendron Store, built in 1929, was the second store in Rhododendron. Maude Krebs reportedly contracted to have this store built. It also housed the post office where she served as postmaster for 30 years. (Courtesy of Nancy Collins.)

Construction of the Mount Hood Highway started in 1922 and roughly followed the route of the Barlow Trail. After completion in 1926, travelers used the highway through Rhododendron to get to Mount Hood. This postcard photograph shows a view of the Zigzag River Bridge and the Mount Hood Loop Highway as it enters Rhododendron with Zigzag Mountain in the background. (Courtesy of Gary Randall.)

This picture is taken from the south end of the Mount Hood Highway at the Zigzag River Bridge looking north. The Rhododendron Inn, which was located just to the east of the bridge, can be seen from this view. The site is where the Rhododendron Footbridge is now located over the Zigzag River. (Courtesy of Gary Randall.)

Portland businessman E. Henry Wemme purchased the rights to what had become known as the Mount Hood and Barlow Road Company in 1912. After Wemme passed away in 1917, the rights were turned over to the Oregon State Highway Commission in 1919. By 1920, the highway commission had modernized the route, better known as the Mount Hood Highway, from Foster Road in Portland, Oregon, to a point two miles east of Government Camp. It did not become the Mount Hood Loop Highway until the completion of the section between Hood River, Oregon, and Government Camp in 1925. The improvements to the highway and the increase in automobile recreation further inspired development in the Hoodland area. This picture shows the construction of the bridge over Still Creek in 1928. (Courtesy of MHCC&M.)

Three

BUSINESSES

In 1908, members of the L.E. (Ludwig) and August (Jabs) Hoffman families settled in Sandy, Oregon. They utilized the knowledge they had gained while living in New York City to open a meat market and butcher shop called the Sandy Market. The store turned out to be the core of a food delivery business serving area housewives and logging camps and eventually delivering to workers in the Civilian Conservation Corps and the Works Progress Administration. They started the business using horse-drawn wagons and upgraded to horsepower-driven trucks. Shown here are Ruben Hoffman with his foot on the running board and Walt Hoffman behind the wheel of one of their new delivery trucks. (Courtesy of the Hoffman family.)

As the community grew and more businesses expanded, the Hoffman brothers opened a second Sandy Market location in Rhododendron to meet the new demands. The Rhododendron Sandy Market was the first in the area to have neon lights and an oil heating stove. Besides being butcher shops, both the Sandy and Rhododendron stores carried general merchandise. They were also experts at fulfilling customers' special orders for items like thimbles, baby bottles, socks, and Forest Service jackets. The Rhododendron and Sandy store personnel took great pride in their ability to provide anything needed by their customers, either wholesale or retail. Name a product and the Sandy Market employees got it. (Courtesy of the Hoffman family, photograph by Gary Randall.)

For many years, the Hoffmans raised their own beef or bought from local ranchers such as the Ten Eycks and Mensingers. Ruben Hoffman, shown here, carved out his own corner of the meat and grocery business by opening the Rhododendron location of the Sandy Market. It was the second location for the Hoffmans. They processed the meat through a slaughterhouse that was located near Ruben Lane in Sandy and kept the best cuts to sell at the Sandy and Rhododendron locations. (Courtesy of the Hoffman family.)

Ruben Hoffman opened the Rhododendron Sandy Market in 1938, selling groceries, general merchandise, and other household items along with the meats. In this 1943 photograph, he is seen with his son Ruben E. (Ed) Hoffman Jr. sitting on his lap. (Courtesy of the Hoffman family.)

Marge Duncan Hoffman was the bookkeeper at the Rhododendron Sandy Market until she married Ruben. She often brought young Ed to the store to visit his father. Here, they are enjoying themselves as Ruben takes a break from the store. (Courtesy of the Hoffman family.)

With increasing tourist traffic traveling to Mount Hood, the business community of Rhododendron grew. In 1942, the Oregon Liquor Control Commission established Liquor Store No. 1115. It was located in the grocery store and soon became one of the most popular businesses in Rhododendron. In 1947, the Hoffmans sold the store to Robert Burton, who only owned the store for two and a half years before selling it to Edwin Gadwood in November 1950. (Courtesy of Gary Randall.)

Maude Krebs had this Rhododendron Store built in the early 1930s. It competed with Hoffman's Sandy Market, which was right next door (to the left in this picture). In addition to general merchandise, this store had a soda fountain and a lunch counter that served hamburgers and homemade pies. In this picture, the US Post Office is located on the far right. Maude Krebs also financed the building of the Log Lodge, which was located directly across the road from this building. (Courtesy of Nancy Collins.)

Looking through the glass French doors of Maude Krebs's Rhododendron Store, the general merchandise for sale and the stools at the soda fountain counter can be seen. This counter was a very popular place for all the kids in town. (Courtesy of Nancy Collins.)

Maude Krebs is pictured standing in the doorway of the Rhododendron US Post Office. She served as postmaster for over 30 years, from February 26, 1930, to November 30, 1960. (Courtesy of Nancy Collins.)

This is Rhododendron as it was in the mid-1950s. Looking down the street, many of the businesses can be seen, including Gadwood's Market, formerly Burton's Market and before that the Rhododendron Sandy Market. Other businesses along this strip included another grocery store, the post office, a bus stop, two service stations, two restaurants, a motel, a greenhouse nursery specializing in begonias, and the area's first fast-food drive-in. (Courtesy of MHCC&M.)

By the 1960s, Gadwood's Market had become the typical country store. The well-worn wooden floors were mended with flattened tin cans nailed over cracks and knot holes, and the shelves were piled high with merchandise of all kinds. Owner Edwin Gadwood even had credit accounts kept on paper ledgers where regular customers could charge their purchases and then settle up at the end of the month. For a short time, there were three cages outside the store where a bear, a raccoon, and a goose were on display for kids to enjoy. Gadwood eventually sold the store to Al Moore, who operated it for a few years until Moore stepped through the well-worn wooden floor and decided it was time to tear the building down and build a new one. (Courtesy of the O'Brien family.)

In 1929, William Lenz, with help from his son Bill, built the Log Lodge for Maude Krebs. The father-son team also built the Barlow Trail Roadhouse; the Travelers Roost, which is now the Zigzag Inn; and several cabins in the area. From the time it was built, the Log Lodge has been an iconic building in Rhododendron. The Log Lodge was a popular restaurant with a long bar and a big dance floor. It was advertised as follows: "The meeting place in Rhododendron with food you will enjoy." It operated as the Log Lodge until approximately 1992, when it opened as Don Guido's Italian Restaurant. Guido's was popular from the day it opened until the day it closed in February 2007. From 2007 until 2019, several other businesses and restaurants called the Log Lodge home, but the building fell into severe disrepair. The building was purchased in 2019 by Anita and Erik Wisloeff-Menteer, who hope to restore it to its former glory. (Courtesy of Nancy Collins.)

This photograph shows two unidentified ladies standing next to the fireplace on the restaurant side of the Log Lodge. Patrons could come in, enjoy a great meal, and sit close to the cozy, warm fireplace after an enjoyable day in the snow. There were two fireplaces, back-to-back. The back side of this fireplace faced the bar and dance floor. (Courtesy of Nancy Collins.)

This photograph shows the spacious dance floor and the second fireplace with a piano in the back corner. Visitors would travel from Portland and join the town regulars to listen to great music and dance the night away with family and friends. (Courtesy of Nancy Collins.)

Bill and Nancy Spencer took over the operation of the Log Lodge from Maude Krebs in 1959, managing the bar and restaurant for seven years. The Spencers were known to be very congenial hosts, and patrons would often drive all the way from Portland to enjoy the great food, generous pours at the bar, dances, and good company. (Courtesy of Nancy Spencer.)

Bill and Nancy Spencer operated the Log Lodge from 1959 until 1966. Bill, shown here behind the bar, was everyone's friend. He loved to talk with his customers and tell jokes. He grew up in Manhattan Beach, California, and attended Pomona College until his schooling was interrupted by World War II. With knowledge he gained while working as an engineer, he moved to Oregon in 1956 and married Nancy Guay in 1958, after they met at Timberline Lodge. In 1959, he left the engineering world to pursue a career in the food and beverage industry. Little did he know that raising two children with Nancy and trying to run a restaurant were more than full-time jobs. Nancy pretty much ran the show behind the scenes. She cooked, cleaned (even though she hated cleaning the men's urinals), greeted guests, and occasionally bartended. Shown here, Nancy is giving Bill a piece of her mind. (Both, courtesy of Nancy Spencer.)

When Bill and Nancy Spencer took over operation of the Log Lodge in 1959, it became the hot spot on the mountain. Nancy served good food at reasonable prices. Bill was the life of the party and was known for pouring liberal drinks. They drew the ski crowds in the winter and the party crowds in the summer. They featured the Mark Allen Players, who periodically performed comedy plays at the lodge. The Spencers did not make much money, but everyone, including them, had a good time. (Courtesy of Nancy Spencer.)

Ethel Gallagher was one of Rhododendron's more colorful personalities. She was single and loved that she was the talk of the town. Dressed to the nines, she would come to the Log Lodge looking to fill her dance card. She owned the Little Holland Café, where she lived in the back. Quite often, she was seen at the café serving breakfast in her bathrobe with curlers in her hair. (Courtesy of Nancy Spencer.)

In many towns, businesses come and go, and Rhododendron was no exception. Wheeler's Handweaving Arts and Crafts was one of many businesses that served Rhododendron over the years. It was located on the north side of Highway 26, just east of the Alpine Begonia Garden. Another business in Rhododendron worth noting was the Washing Well. It was located on the south side of Highway 26 and was a coin-operated laundry business built by Bill and Eileen Anderson in the 1960s. After a major fire in the 1970s, it was rebuilt to later become a gun shop, then an antique store, and in 2016, the building opened as a cannabis shop. A few other businesses in Rhododendron that have come and gone include a dental office/duplex that was built and operated by Dr. William Gulick and later purchased by Dr. Frank Strange, who then converted it into a triplex; two real estate companies, Spencer Realty and S&A Real Estate; as well as the Little Holland Café; Mountain Chowder House; the Turquoise Trader; and Bartley's Plumbing and Welding. (Courtesy of Gary Randall.)

Pat Aeppli is shown here holding her daughter Christie near the Rhododendron Post Office. Communities were identified by their post office. The first post office, established on February 23, 1909, identified the community as Rowe, Oregon. It was located in Dad Miller's store, with Lee Holden serving as the first postmaster. On February 27, 1917, the Rowe Post Office was relocated down the road to the Gateway and renamed the Zigzag Post Office. (Courtesy of Bill White, photograph by the Aeppli family.)

Prior to 1920, Rhododendron was known as Rowe, Oregon, in honor of former Portland mayor Henry S. Rowe, who in 1909 opened the Rhododendron Inn. The Rowe Post Office was moved several times and renamed the Zigzag Post Office in 1917. On January 26, 1920, the US Postal Service established a new post office, officially naming it the Rhododendron Post Office to celebrate the native rhododendrons that are prolific in the area. The area has been known as Rhododendron, Oregon, ever since. (Courtesy of Bill White.)

In 1959, Dale and Edna Lamoreaux opened the Sno Bird Drive-In. The photographs show the back of the drive-in on opening day and a side view with customers. The property was originally owned by Edna Lamoreaux's maternal grandfather, Howard Pew, who passed it on to his daughter Wyola and her husband, Clark Miles. In 1959, Clark Miles gave his son-in-law Dale Lamoreaux an acre of land to develop along Highway 26. Dale built the Sno Bird Drive-In, which was located where the Dairy Queen parking lot is today. In the early 1970s, Dale sold it to Bill and Meredith Closner, who ran it as the Sno Bird for a few years after adding some indoor seating. The Closners sold the restaurant in 1977 to the Lunstrums, who then sold it to Bob and Jan Peters in 1979. (Both, courtesy of the Lamoreaux family.)

After the Sno Bird Drive-In was sold to Bob and Jan Peters in 1979, they purchased a Dairy Queen franchise and added the mansard roof and the drive-through window to comply with Dairy Queen's franchise specifications. (Courtesy of Melinda Minch.)

In 1982, Bob Peters sold the Dairy Queen to his sister Gail and her husband, Cary Vincent. For a short time, the Vincents partnered with their daughter Melinda and her husband, Dan Minch. In 1986, the Minchs took over sole ownership. In 1993, the new Dairy Queen, shown here, was built, and the old Dairy Queen was demolished to make room for the parking lot. In 2018, Angela (Minch) Harrell and her husband, Zack Harrell, purchased ownership of the business from her parents. (Courtesy of Melinda Minch.)

The Alpine Begonia Garden was a fixture in Rhododendron for many years. Built by May and Albert Closner in the 1950s, it was a nursery that specialized in begonias and rhododendrons. Eventually falling into disrepair, it was torn down to make room for the widening of Highway 26. The Dairy Queen now sits on the site of the old Alpine Begonia Garden. (Courtesy of Elaine Hagen.)

As the tourist trade continued to increase, so did the number of restaurants and cafés. Over the years, the area saw many eating establishments come and go. Pictured here is the sign identifying Don Pablo's, a once-popular restaurant featuring Mexican cuisine. It was located in a small cabin just east of Rhododendron at Bell Lake Road that was built by John Lake Sr. as a grocery store for the 1959 Oregon Trail Centennial. (Courtesy of John Lake.)

The Snowline Motel was originally known as the Evergreen Cabins. The motel consisted of five Steiner-built log cabins constructed in the 1930s and four duplexes built in the early 1940s. The duplexes and two of the log cabins were situated along the Zigzag River and were used as short-term rentals for visitors vacationing in Rhododendron. In 1944, Alan B. Olson and his wife, Catherine, moved to Rhododendron from Bismarck, North Dakota. They bought the Evergreen Cabins shortly after moving to town and managed them until selling in 1951. The 10-unit motel portion was built by the new owners in the early 1950s, and the name was changed to the Snowline Motel. (Courtesy of Steven Kenney.)

Here is the original Alpine Hut restaurant. Built sometime in the 1940s, it served as Rhododendron's main breakfast, lunch, and dinner café. Fred Walsh was the owner until 1954, when Marie Hagen bought the business and the building. She was quite the businesswoman and ran the Alpine Hut until 1960, when her son Jim Henry took over. Jim had worked for his mother at the restaurant through high school and knew the business well. (Courtesy of Elaine Hagen.)

In 1964, the original Alpine Hut was replaced with the new Alpine Hut. The old building was bulldozed to make room for the parking lot and Highway 26 expansion. (Courtesy of Elaine Hagen.)

It was a sad day in 1964 when crews demolished the first Alpine Hut to make way for the new building's parking lot. The new, improved Alpine Hut was built behind the original so the restaurant could stay open during deconstruction. (Courtesy of Elaine Hagen.)

Side-by-side comparisons show the two Alpine Hut coffee shops. Both the old building and the new building separated the coffee shops from the dining rooms. The Alpine Hut coffee shops were very popular with the local folks as well as with people traveling through Rhododendron. (Both, courtesy of Elaine Hagen.)

The Alpine Hut bar in the original building was a popular and comfortable place for the locals to gather. Here, Robert Albertson is sitting on the stool with his wife, Elizabeth, standing behind him. Their daughter Marie Hagen, owner of the Alpine Hut, is also behind the bar with her son Jim Henry and former owner Fred Walsh. The Albertsons were frequent visitors. (Courtesy of Elaine Hagen.)

Pictured here is the bar area in the second Alpine Hut. The bartender serving area was sunken to make for a better face-to-face experience with patrons sitting at the counter. The Alpine Hut bar was very popular with the golf crowd. (Courtesy of Elaine Hagen.)

Side-by-side comparisons of the Alpine Hut dining rooms show how important a cozy fireplace figured in each room. With the noisy coffee shops off to one end of each building, the dining rooms offered a warm fire and a quiet atmosphere for fine dining and casual conversation. (Both, courtesy of Elaine Hagen.)

Jim Henry took over the operation of the Alpine Hut from his mother in 1964. Pictured here, Jim is playing a game of shuffleboard in the original Alpine Hut, cheered on by an unidentified observer. (Courtesy of Elaine Hagen.)

Chef Craig Calvert purchased the Alpine Hut from Jim Henry in 1984. As owner, chef, and manager, Craig was often found working in the kitchen or serving drinks to the golf crowd from behind the bar. (Courtesy of Craig Calvert.)

As a point of reference for this photograph, the person on the left is standing in the west parking lot of the Log Lodge. Located across the highway is the original Alpine Hut restaurant, and just to the right of that, a corner of the Alpine Begonia Garden can be seen. (Courtesy of Elaine Hagen.)

Glen Asher owned the Barlow Trail Furniture Shops in Rhododendron. He made custom furniture for many of the local residents and also for the Zigzag Inn. The shop was located just to the east of the Log Lodge, and his home was next to the shop behind the Log Lodge. Here, he is seen with his two young daughters, Tessa Ann and Elaine, on his lap. (Courtesy of Elaine Hagen.)

This is Glen Asher (left) in his shop with his brother Don, who worked with him. They made a great team and ran the shop from about 1945 to 1955. Glen was not only an expert woodworker, he was also an expert mountaineer, having climbed Mount Hood 59 times. His claim to fame was climbing to the top of all Three Sisters mountains in central Oregon within 24 hours. (Courtesy of Elaine Hagen.)

Glen's furniture company advertisement, shown here, was very simple. (Courtesy of MHCC&M.)

This is an example of the fine workmanship of Glen and Don Asher. This table set is on display at the Mount Hood Cultural Center and Museum in Government Camp. (Courtesy of MHCC&M.)

In 1955, Glen Asher decided to close up shop and move to Portland to raise his family. Joie Smith then moved into his building, where she opened her first ski shop. Pictured across the highway from the tractor plowing snow is Glen Asher's building with the "Joie's Ski Shop" sign featured across the front. (Courtesy of Elaine Hagen.)

Joie originally opened her ski shop in Glen Asher's furniture building after he moved out. In 1959, after her business became more successful, Joie moved her shop down the road into this vacated Pioneer Supply building. Built in 1929, it was used as a plumbing supply warehouse prior to Joie moving in. (Courtesy of Bill White.)

Alpine Towing owner Joie Smith was notable throughout the Hoodland area. For nearly 50 years, Joie and her fleet of tow trucks rescued many snow-stranded vehicles and untangled many serious accidents. Here, one of her heavy haulers is assisting with the delivery of a new Hoodland fire truck. (Courtesy of Bill White.)

In the early 1960s, Joie Smith realized that the area needed more tow truck services, so in 1967, she converted her ski shop and opened Alpine Towing. She operated the business 24 hours a day, seven days a week. From her home, which was located in the woods not far from the shop, she would monitor many emergency radio frequencies, listening for calls requesting assistance. She would rush over to her shop, hop into a rig, and quite often she would be the first responder to emergency situations, long before other emergency personnel got to the scene. (Courtesy of Bill White.)

As automobile travel to and from Mount Hood increased, so did the need for gas and repair stations. Rhododendron had two full-service garages. They were basically across the highway from each other and often competed for business. The Chevron Standard Service Station, pictured above, replaced George Crabb's Red Crown Garage, pictured below. Both were gathering places for some of the local men. They would sit outside the stations and play cribbage for hours. (Above, courtesy of Elaine Hagen; below, courtesy of Gary Randall.)

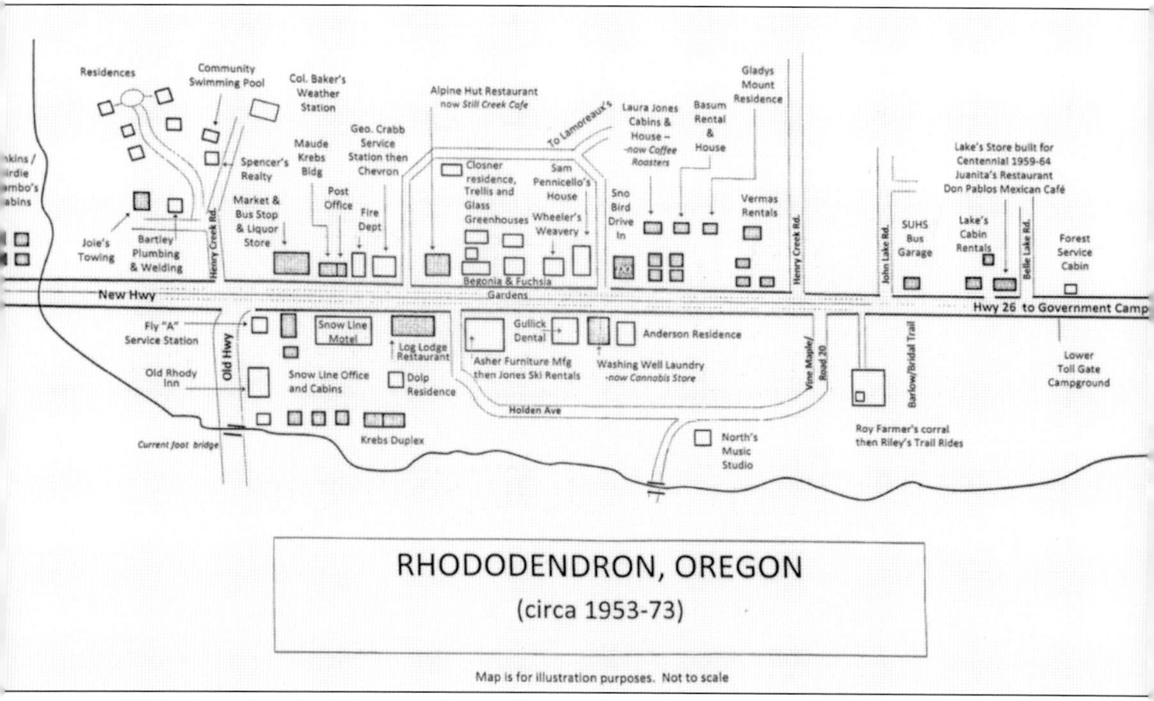

In 2020, when the Rhododendron Post Office celebrated its centennial, John Lake, who was born in 1943 and has lived in Rhododendron all his life, drew this map of the town. His map shows the locations of many of the businesses that served Rhododendron over the years. (Courtesy of John Lake.)

Four

Movers, Shakers, and Other Characters of Rhododendron

Emil and Susette Franzetti bought the Rhododendron Inn from Henry S. Rowe in 1912. In 1916, Emil was killed when his automobile accidentally overturned near the Zigzag Ranger Station. For seven years, Susette ran the inn by herself and then sold it along with six acres to William Cash. Susette was quite the businesswoman. She had her remaining land surveyed, divided into building lots, and recorded with Clackamas County as the Franzetti Addition. She then contracted with Henry Steiner to build several speculative cabins and sold them to new owners. Because of her, many Steiner cabins exist in the Rhododendron area. (Courtesy of OHS.)

Joie Emilie Smith was born on June 17, 1928, in the Mount Tabor/Laurelhurst area of Portland, Oregon, to June (Reid) and Oscar Clossett. After Oscar's passing, her mother married Blasdel Smith, who adopted Joie. In 1953, she moved to Rhododendron, where she became an icon and was best known for operating a ski shop and Alpine Towing. (Courtesy of Matt Reid.)

Since childhood, Joie had a passion for horses. She spent much of her younger years at her parents' pony barn in southeast Portland. Her dad bought her a pony named Danny Boy, which she would ride all the way from southeast Portland to Camp Namanu east of the Sandy River. (Courtesy of Matt Reid.)

While attending the University of Oregon, Joie discovered two compelling interests, flying and skiing. She used money from selling one of her horses to take flying lessons. After only four hours of instruction, she took her first solo flight in an F2B Funk. Over the ensuing years, she became certified to fly many different types of small aircraft. (Courtesy of Matt Reid.)

Joie Smith was well known in the Mount Hood area for over 50 years. She learned to ski while accompanying her father on his visits to Timberline after it opened in 1937. During high school, she learned that ski patrol members could ski free, so she rapidly applied. After joining the Mount Hood Ski Patrol, she became a member of the National Ski Patrol. (Courtesy of Matt Reid.)

Joie Smith attended the University of Oregon for two years and then transferred to Vanport College, now Portland State University. She majored in mechanical engineering and earned an upper division certificate in engineering in the late 1940s. (Courtesy of Matt Reid.)

Skiing was a passion for Joie, who often raced competitively. In 1951, she participated in the National Alpine Ski Races. She would have been an Olympic contender had it not been for breaking her leg in a grisly skiing accident in 1955 during the Golden Rose Ski Classic at Timberline. After a year recuperating, she started skiing again but not competitively. She was a member of the Mount Hood Ski Patrol and one of only five women on the 85-member ski patrol for the 1960 Winter Olympics in Squaw Valley, California. (Courtesy of MHCC&M.)

Joie opened her own ski shop in 1955, making a business out of something she loved. Joie's Ski Shop was very profitable for several years. But, after a burglary at the shop, along with her dislike for the newfangled plastic skis and the widening of Highway 26, she closed the ski shop. Needing another way to make a living on the mountain led her to opening Alpine Towing in 1967. (Courtesy of Gary Randall.)

Joie Smith never owned a piece of equipment she could not operate. In 1967, she started Alpine Towing after purchasing a one-ton 1956 Ford truck with a homemade tow apparatus. Her company was one of only two towing companies between Cherryville and Warm Springs. Joie had plenty of business and was often a first responder to accidents on the mountain. Eventually, her fleet grew to seven trucks, two caterpillars, and a track hoe excavator. (Courtesy of Bill White.)

Joie Smith loved working for herself. From starting a ski shop to running a heavy-haul towing business, she kept busy helping anyone in need on the mountain. When not rescuing someone, she would relax by riding one of several horses she corralled at her home on Henry Creek Road. Until she passed away on March 29, 2014, Joie remained active in the community. (Courtesy of Matt Reid.)

In the summer of 1960, Joie Smith and her good friend Carol Haugk rode their horses down Henry Creek Road. Carol admired a tiny log cabin built right into Zigzag Mountain. In 1963, Carol moved into that tiny cabin with her husband, Steve, and one-month-old daughter, Barbara. (Courtesy of Barbara and Carol Haugk.)

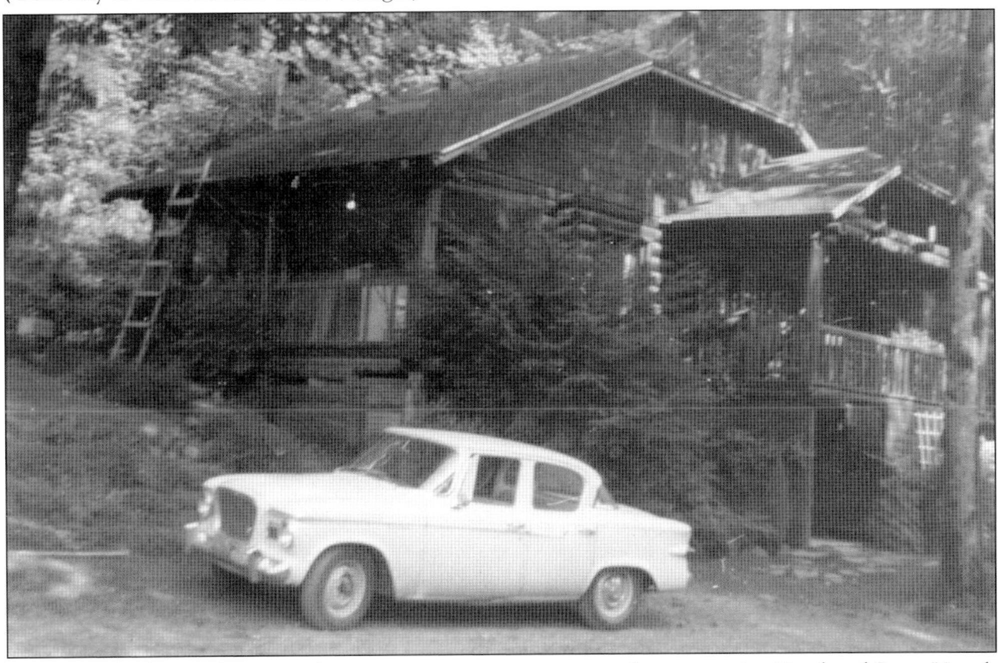

Like many of the employees working in various occupations on the mountain, Carol and Steve Haugk made Rhododendron their home. They extensively remodeled their tiny cabin while both worked full time at Timberline Lodge. The only remaining logs from the original cabin are the ceiling logs on the main floor. Today, the cabin has four times the original living space. Since retiring from Timberline, Carol has remained active in the community. (Courtesy of Barbara and Carol Haugk.)

From 1905 to 1908, Arlie Mitchell served as the last gatekeeper at Tollgate No. 5 in Rhododendron. He was 19 years old when he started as gatekeeper. This photograph shows Arlie, at 88 years old, standing by the commemorative sign honoring the last tollgate on the Barlow Road. In the background is a replica of the gate and one of the two original big leaf maple trees that were planted by Daniel Parker, a tollgate keeper prior to 1905. The maple trees have been recognized as Oregon State Heritage Trees. (Courtesy of MHCC&M.)

Arlie Mitchell entered the US Navy on July 10, 1917, at the age of 31 and served for three years. During his time in the Navy, he crossed the Atlantic Ocean from New York to Europe 12 times. He did two years of foreign service in England, Ireland, Scotland, Wales, and France. (Courtesy of Rebecca Copley.)

Arlie and Anna (Ringnes) Mitchell were married on August 18, 1928, at Anna's mother's home in Canby, Oregon. They met while Anna was teaching at Welches Grade School. They were a bit older when they married: Arlie was 42, and Anna was 34. (Courtesy of Rebecca Copley.)

Arlie Edward Mitchell and Anna (Ringnes) Mitchell are standing by the outdoor fireplace that Arlie and his son Ed built as part of Ed's 4-H Home Beautification project. Arlie was born on December 6, 1886, in Sandy, Oregon. Anna was born on January 30, 1894, in Canby, Oregon. Arlie was one of nine children born to Steven and Ellen Mitchell. Arlie and Anna lived their entire married life in the same house on Pinner Road in the Faubion area near Rhododendron. (Courtesy of Rebecca Copley.)

Even though Arlie only completed school through the eighth grade, he was always studying and learning new things. When his daughter took piano lessons, he taught himself to read music and to play the piano. He loved poetry and would frequently read to his grandchildren. They would sit on his lap, and he would recite poetry or tell them a story. Grandson Paul is on Anna's lap, granddaughter Rebecca is standing, and Arlie is holding their grandson Steve. (Courtesy of Rebecca Copley.)

Arlie built this house on Pinner Road in 1923, before he and Anna married. They were beginning to think they would never have children. But, in 1936, their daughter, Ellen, was born, and in 1937, they welcomed their son, Edward. They had cribs in their parents' bedroom until Arlie finished an addition to the house. It included a back porch with an indoor bathroom, a laundry room with a wringer washer, and a second story with two bedrooms for the children. Arlie would rescue broken skis from Government Camp or Timberline Lodge, repairing them for his kids to use. Ellen and Edward loved to ski right out the front door of their house. Some years, it would snow so much that they could ski over the top of the fence. (Both, courtesy of Rebecca Copley.)

In 1885, William John Lenz was born in The Dalles, Oregon. He and his twin brother, Joseph, were raised in Hood River, Oregon. After moving his family to Zigzag in 1922, William built several distinctive log buildings, including the Barlow Trail Inn in 1926, the Zigzag Inn in 1927, and the Log Lodge in 1929. He also helped build the first Mazama Lodge on Mount Hood near Government Camp, as well as many custom homes in Mountain Air Park and in the surrounding area. He was also known for building artisan custom furniture. (Courtesy of Gary Lenz.)

Posing for a family picture around 1920 are William Lenz, his wife, Helen, and their daughter Donna and son Bill. William was a self-taught musician. He loved to play the guitar and to write music. He also loved the outdoors and would often hike and ski Lolo Pass to Hood River to visit his parents. (Courtesy of Gary Lenz.)

William Lenz is hand-peeling logs for his next project. Besides building log structures and artisan furniture, he loved the outdoors. He was an avid hiker and an often-requested guide on Mount Hood. He also enjoyed hunting deer, elk, bear, and cougar. As a natural mathematician, and without any formal training, he drew beautiful blueprints. (Courtesy of Gary Lenz.)

Just like his father, William Lenz Jr., or Bill as he preferred to be called, was an avid outdoorsman. He was born in a little village near Hood River called Mount Hood, Oregon, on September 18, 1915. When he was seven, the family moved to the Zigzag area, where he attended Welches Grade School and graduated from Sandy High School. Being an excellent skier, snowshoer, and athlete, he climbed Mount Hood six times during his lifetime. Although he helped his father build the Log Lodge and the Zigzag Inn, in 1952, he began working for Portland General Electric, where he later became an outside foreman. (Both, courtesy of Gary Lenz.)

The Pew/Miles/Lamoreaux family has resided in Rhododendron since purchasing a portion of the Heinrich Haman homestead and cabin from Susette Franzetti in 1923. This photograph, taken in July 1939, shows Howard and Ada Pew celebrating their 50th wedding anniversary on the Pew/Miles/Lamoreaux property. Their daughter Wyola (Pew) Miles is in the center wearing the white dress, and Howard and Ada are to the left of her. Kneeling in front are, from left to right, Wyola's daughter Edna, who later married Dale Lamoreaux, and Wyola's sister Alta Pew. Standing behind Howard and Ada are unidentified extended family members. (Courtesy of the Lamoreaux family.)

The Lamoreaux cabin, built in 1903 by Heinrich Haman, has remained in the family since it was purchased by Howard and Ada Pew in 1923. This picture, taken in the early 1920s, shows the exterior of the homestead after the front and side sleeping porches were added. The fireplace and chimney, originally in the middle of the house, were moved to one end. Michelle Lamoreaux currently owns the home and is a full-time resident of Rhododendron. (Courtesy of the Lamoreaux family.)

Taken in 1959, this picture of the Lamoreaux girls with their mom, Edna, shows them waiting on the sunny porch of their home for pancakes, probably being made by their dad, Dale. From left to right are Sharon, Renee (sitting on Edna's lap), and Michelle. Their younger brother, David, was born several years after this photograph was taken. (Courtesy of the Lamoreaux family.)

The John Lake family became longtime residents of Rhododendron after moving from Orient, Oregon, in 1945. John Herman Lake was born on June 26, 1906, and married Belle Newlands in 1940. John worked at a forest fire lookout for 17 years and also worked in logging and home construction. The Lake family was well known throughout the area. John and Belle's boys worked at Multorpor and Ski Bowl, helping construct many of the ski lifts. John Sr. was renowned for building many of the summer homes in the area. Belle Lake is seen here holding their youngest child, Bill, born in 1946. Bill was tragically killed in an automobile accident in 1969 at the age of 23. Standing in front of her are sons Charlie (left), born in 1941, and John Jr., born in 1943. John Jr. still lives on the property where he grew up. (Courtesy of John Lake.)

The house in the background is where the Lake boys grew up. It was built by their dad, John Herman Lake. A fish pond in the back was stocked with rainbow trout and two sturgeons. John called them their pets. In the early 1900s, their paternal grandfather, John Howard Lake, and their dad, John Herman Lake, would drive this old wagon to Wamic for grocery supplies. (Courtesy of John Lake.)

Taken when his boys were very young, this photograph is of the house built by John Herman Lake. Over time, the chimney became covered in ivy. Years later, John Jr. removed the ivy and discovered a face with a pipe in its mouth on the exterior of the chimney. Apparently, his dad had built the face into the chimney and designed it so that when a fire burned in the fireplace, smoke would come out of the pipe, making it look like the face was smoking. (Courtesy of John Lake.)

In 1979, Michael P. Jones founded the nonprofit Cascade Geographic Society. Its purpose was to document the cultural, historical, and natural resources of the Cascade Mountain Range. On his property in Rhododendron, he and his wife, Nita Kreuzer, have hosted a variety of annual events, including the Mount Hood Huckleberry Festival, the Salmon and Mushroom Festival, the Heritage Quilt Show, and Christmas along the Oregon Trail. (Courtesy of Nita Kreuzer.)

Michael P. Jones and his wife, Nita Kreuzer, assisted by a large group of volunteers, hosted annual events like the Heritage Quilt Show, which featured handmade heirloom quilts as well as new quilts made by local artisans. Other annual events were held in the historical area called the Oregon Country Settlement, which is located behind the Alpine Hut. Pioneer-themed buildings have been reconstructed or refurbished, bringing to life the rich pioneer atmosphere that had a ubiquitous influence over the growth of Rhododendron. (Courtesy of Nita Kreuzer.)

Forest and Juanita Anliker were well known in Rhododendron. Forest was the epitome of a mountain man. Working in the woods as a tree faller most of his life, he was strong as an ox but gentle as a lamb. If Rhododendron residents ever needed a tree taken down, Forest was the man they called. Forest worked in construction and for a logging company, commuting from their home in Hillsboro until he moved his family to Rhododendron in 1959. He then started Forest's Tree Service, taking down trees and delivering firewood all while continuing his work as a carpenter. He was still felling (and topping) trees until his early 70s. His wife, Juanita, besides raising two sons (Fred and Gary) and a daughter (Karen), is best known for working at Gadwood's Market for both Ed Gadwood and Al Moore. (Courtesy of the Anliker family.)

Five

Camps, Cabins, and Cottages

The Loop Inn Campground was located approximately where the Zigzag Ranger Station is today. Many stage services stopped here to let riders stretch their legs and maybe purchase a nice cold beverage before continuing the journey to Government Camp and beyond. (Courtesy of Steven Kenney.)

In the early days, the drive to Rhododendron took anywhere from one to three days. Often, the trip included a picnic along the way. This group has stopped for lunch on the way to Rhododendron. (Courtesy of Gary Randall.)

The Rhododendron Inn offered tent camping, which was popular in the Mount Hood area. The inn offered sites along with tents that could be rented for a week, a month, or for an entire summer. Renters could enjoy all of the activities and meals offered by the inn. Tent sites could also be purchased outright. Some families would stake out similar campsites on nearby national forest land where they would return every summer. (Courtesy of Gary Randall.)

Camp Rusty was one of the first cabins in Rhododendron. Built in 1914 by Phillip Buebke with help from his 90-year-old father-in-law, James Brady, it was named after Buebke's wife, Mame, for her rust-colored red hair. Standing in front of the completed cabin are members of the Buebke family. Phillip is second from the left, and James, with the long beard, is standing next to him. (Courtesy of Anne Leu Kuzminski.)

This cabin replaced Camp Rusty after the original was destroyed by fire. It remains in the family, serving five generations of Buebke, Leu, and Kuzminski families. The cabin is located at the corner of Road 10, which was once part of the Barlow Road and then the Mount Hood Loop Highway, and East Marion Road. East Marion Road is also known by some as Moon Crater Road because of its numerous potholes. Marion was Phillip and Mame Buebke's only child, and Marion Road is named after her. (Courtesy of Anne Leu Kuzminski.)

Phillip Buebke, who built Camp Rusty in 1914, was born in Germany and came to the United States when he was a teenager. He started Columbia Wire and Iron Works in Portland. Camp Rusty still has many examples of his ironwork. The Buebkes were very good friends with Susette Franzetti and hosted her on many holidays. (Courtesy of Anne Leu Kuzminski.)

The not-so-secret Still Creek swimming hole has attracted generations of swimmers, like these children shown in 1917. Many braved the cold, glacial, spring-fed waters as youngsters to prove their toughness to the older generation. Still Creek was also known for its rainbow and cutthroat trout. Salmon and steelhead trout can be seen returning to spawn in the creek every September and October. (Courtesy of Anne Leu Kuzminski.)

This photograph shows a typical outdoor dinner party at the original Camp Rusty. From left to right are Mame, Marion, and Phillip Buebke enjoying an afternoon with family. Phillip's brother is pouring a glass of beer for Alice, Mame's sister. The table and benches were made by the Buebke family from material found on the property. (Courtesy of Anne Leu Kuzminski.)

Pictured here are friends enjoying the day playing in Still Creek. Standing in the back left with her arm around young Marion Buebke is Anne Dempsey, who was Marion's cousin and the daughter of the famous Nonpareil Jack Dempsey (not to be confused with the other prize fighter Jack Dempsey). Anne was a nurse during World War I and one of the first women to scale Mount Hood. (Courtesy of Anne Leu Kuzminski.)

The Farrington House, built in 1929, is still enjoyed by members of the family. It is distinctive because of the charming rock work that made up the foundation and retaining walls. The home is located where Still Creek (shown here) and the Zigzag River join just west of Rhododendron. Both Still Creek and the Zigzag River were dramatically changed during the flood of 1964. Unfortunately, much of the beautiful rock work that is shown on the left of this photograph was destroyed in that flood. (Courtesy of Doug Crane.)

This photograph, taken in August 1929, shows one of the first nights the Farrington family spent in their new summer home. The chandelier and many of the light fixtures were designed using fungus found in the old-growth forest. Much of the furniture was built from the trees that were cut down to make room for the cabin. All were designed by Samuel Lancaster, who was the head engineer on the original Columbia River Highway. (Courtesy of Doug Crane.)

When the Forest Service created summer home tracts, it elected to incorporate some of the sites that had been used for years as family campsites. Families were given first choice to lease their old campsite. One of those was the Farrington family. Here, they are posing for their family reunion in 1930 on the portico of their new summer home. This home was designed by Samuel Lancaster, the engineer who designed the famed historic Columbia River Highway. The stone arches on the porch are the signature design of Lancaster, and similar arches can be found along many parts of the scenic highway. The same Italian rock masons who worked on the highway and Timberline Lodge also built the rock porch for the Farrington family's summer home. (Courtesy of Doug Crane.)

James Walter Creighton, son of William H. and Cynthia, with his wife, Elsie, homesteaded in Rhododendron. Their property was located just west of the confluence of Still Creek and Zigzag River along the Mount Hood Loop Highway. It was eventually donated to the Girl Scouts and is known today as the Homestead. (Courtesy of the Girl Scouts.)

Walter Creighton, as he preferred to be called, was the last person to be granted a homestead in the Oregon National Forest, now known as the Mount Hood National Forest. He built a small two-room cabin in 1910 before he filed for his homestead claim in 1912. His claim was granted in 1919 by Pres. Woodrow Wilson. In 1922, Walter built this large, two-story modern house with high-quality milled lumber that still remains in good condition. Walter was a contract builder of homes and barns in the community. His buildings stand out in this forest community, as they differ from the more common rustic style of other cabins in the area. (Courtesy of the Girl Scouts.)

In 1968, the Homestead property was willed to the Girls Scouts by Walter and Elsie Creighton, as they had no children of their own. The Creightons wanted to preserve a place where children could see big trees, because Walter thought in another 15 years or so there would not be any left to enjoy. This property is now used by the Girl Scouts as a day camp, but it is also offered to the public as a rental. The turnaround at the Creighton Homestead shows some of the equipment that Walter used for his work as a logger, carpenter, plumber, hunter, and fisherman. He was also in charge of the Rhododendron water system for several years. But most people knew him for his ability to raise coon hounds. He raised his first litter of dogs when he was eight years old. He entered his dogs into competitions everywhere on the Pacific coast. Because his hounds were so superior in their class, he gave up exhibiting them due to the lack of competition. (Courtesy of the Girl Scouts.)

Henry Steiner was a local cabin builder and contractor known for his fine craftsmanship and use of local materials. He never bought anything that he could make himself. Born in 1877, he married Amalia "Molly" Jaster in 1905. Building cabins was a family affair, as all of Henry and Molly's 13 children contributed in some way to the process. The boys, John and Fred, cleared the land, cut trees into logs, and shaved cedar trees into shingles. The girls hand peeled the logs. Since there was no electricity, they primarily used manual tools for construction, but with necessity being the mother of invention, they somehow fashioned a 1930 Ford Model AA flatbed truck into a makeshift table saw. Wielding a 16-pound sledgehammer, John, the stronger son, could turn giant boulders into flat-faced rocks used for chimneys and fireplaces that he would build. Henry Steiner died on April 7, 1953, while out hunting in the forest he loved. Four days later, on April 11, 1953, his son Fred drowned in the Sandy River while out searching for his missing father. (Courtesy of MHCC&M.)

John William Steiner, born on November 27, 1912, was the fifth of 13 children born to Henry and Molly Steiner. He met Frances Brewer at the Brightwood Tavern. She was a cowgirl turned welder turned bartender when she met John. They were married in 1948 and were living in Rhododendron when their first child, Richard, was born. Their second child, Kerry, was born in 1952. John worked well beyond retirement, building many homes from Government Camp to the Oregon coast. He continued building well into his 80s before finally slowing down. John Steiner passed away on April 13, 2012. (Courtesy of MHCC&M.)

During the late 1920s and into the late 1940s, Henry Steiner, along with his two sons, John and Fred, constructed over 100 log homes, mostly in the Rhododendron and Mount Hood area. Steiner utilized logs harvested from each property site and built unique cabins that have lasted generations. A Steiner signature design incorporated either a sunburst or a cross over each cabin's entryway. He also used interestingly shaped limbs and branches as unique handrails or door knobs. This cabin was built in 1932 by the Steiners as a "spec" cabin for Susette Franzetti to show to prospective lot purchasers. Elsie Bradt, a Portland, Oregon, motion picture theater owner, purchased this cabin in 1932 for $600. William and Eda Graeper, owners of Graeper's Egyptian Theater in Northeast Portland, were fellow theater owners and frequently visited Bradt at the cabin. In 1942, when Graeper approached Bradt with an offer to purchase her theater, she turned him down but offered to sell him the cabin. Graeper Sr. immediately turned to his son and partner, William Graeper Jr., and said, "William, you're buying this cabin." Bradt sold the cabin to William and Ruth Graeper in 1942 for $1,500, and the Graepers have been proud owners ever since. The sign over the porch prominently displays the cabin name Still Th'Air. The name is a play on words coined by Ruth Graeper's mother, Tina Rudd, who on her second visit to see the cabin exclaimed, "Whelp, it's still there!" (Courtesy of Gary Randall.)

Like many of the camps, cabins, and cottages in and around Rhododendron, multiple generations of family members have enjoyed the relaxing atmosphere, the solitude, the peace, the quiet, and the warm comfort offered by visiting or living in the forests. Pictured here is Steve and Judi Graeper's granddaughter Sawyer Rae Stanfill walking into the family cabin Still Th'Air for her very first time. It was the beginning of many fond memories that she will cherish forever. (Authors' collection.)

John Steiner, standing at right on the porch with Steve, visited the Graeper cabin in 2008. He was 96 years old. When Steiner was asked if he remembered when his dad built this cabin, he emphatically said, "My dad, Hell! I built this cabin and I remember every goddamned nail in the place!" (Authors' collection.)

This Steiner cabin was built between 1930 and 1931 on a lot that was part of the Franzetti Addition. The Franzetti Addition was created in the late 1920s when Susette Franzetti subdivided her property and sold lots on which summer cabins could be built. The Franzetti Addition contains the majority of the privately owned properties in Rhododendron. (Courtesy of the O'Brien family.)

The Nizic/O'Brien/Gorman cabin, built by the Steiners, is known throughout the neighborhood as the Three Sisters. Purchased by Samuel and Harriet Nizic in 1943 for $1,800, the cabin was named to honor his three daughters. They are, from left to right, Barbara Nizic, who married Jack O'Brien; Harriet Nizic, who married Tom Gorman; and Sr. Pat Nizic, Sisters of the Holy Names of Jesus and Mary. The extended families of the sisters continue to enjoy the family cabin. (Courtesy of O'Brien family.)

Located just off Road 20 at Marion Road in Rhododendron is the Sign Tree. Many owners of Forest Service and privately owned cabins in the area have named their cabins. Prior to the county assigning street addresses, cabin locations were often referenced by lot number, Forest Service road number, and cabin name. Forest Service cabins still primarily use lot and road numbers for identification. (Courtesy Mike and Lyn Miskowicz.)

Nancy Dougherty, a Welches schoolteacher, purchased this cabin in the 1960s. It was severely run-down, but she restored it and then asked the Mount Hood Cultural Center and Museum to help her inventory and document the history of these outstanding examples of Oregon rustic architecture. Over 100 Steiner cabins have been documented, 30 of which are located in Rhododendron. The museum holds an annual tour of these iconic cabins and continues to promote their preservation. (Courtesy of MHCC&M.)

This is a stunning example of a larger Steiner cabin. It features a bridge across the living room to access the bedrooms on the second floor. The Steiners only built this unique feature into a few of their cabins. (Courtesy of MHCC&M.)

This picture of a Steiner cabin interior shows a bridge across the living room. The use of natural wood logs provides rich warmth and creates the sense of a cozy, relaxed atmosphere, which is common in all Steiner-built cabins. (Courtesy of MHCC&M.)

In the early 1930s, George and Linda Atiyeh, parents of Oregon governor Victor Atiyeh, rented a house in Rhododendron for several summers. It had no electricity and no heat except for the fireplace and a woodstove in the kitchen. When they bought the house in 1936, they remodeled it and added a new kitchen, a dining room, and a downstairs bedroom and bathroom. Roscoe Hemingway, a prominent Portland architect, designed the remodel. The house is still enjoyed by the extended Atiyeh family. (Courtesy of the Atiyeh family.)

This picture of Gov. Victor Atiyeh was taken when he was about 12 years old. He and his twin brothers, Edward and Richard, spent many summers at the cabin on the Zigzag River. Victor always enjoyed fishing whenever he was there. Victor married Delores Hewitt and had two children. He served as Oregon's governor from 1979 to 1987 and passed away in 2014. (Courtesy of the Atiyeh family.)

Wilbur and Evelyn Reid's Alderbrook Lodge was the first summer home built in Rowe (Rhododendron), Oregon. It was built by Wilbur Reid in 1912 for his new wife, Evelyn, whom he first met at the Rhododendron Inn when their families were guests. This American Craftsman and Prairie School–style home overlooks the Zigzag River. It is the only home in the Rhododendron area listed in the National Register of Historic Places. (Courtesy of Matt Reid.)

In this picture, Wilbur Reid and friends are gathered on the banks of the Zigzag River enjoying an afternoon while staying at Alderbrook Lodge. Standing on the rock to the right is Wilbur Reid with his soon-to-be wife, Evelyn. Having met as children at the Rhododendron Inn when both of their parents were summering at Mount Hood, they fell in love and were married in 1914. Standing between them is Evelyn's sister, Zola. The people sitting on the rock are unidentified friends or family. (Courtesy of Matt Reid.)

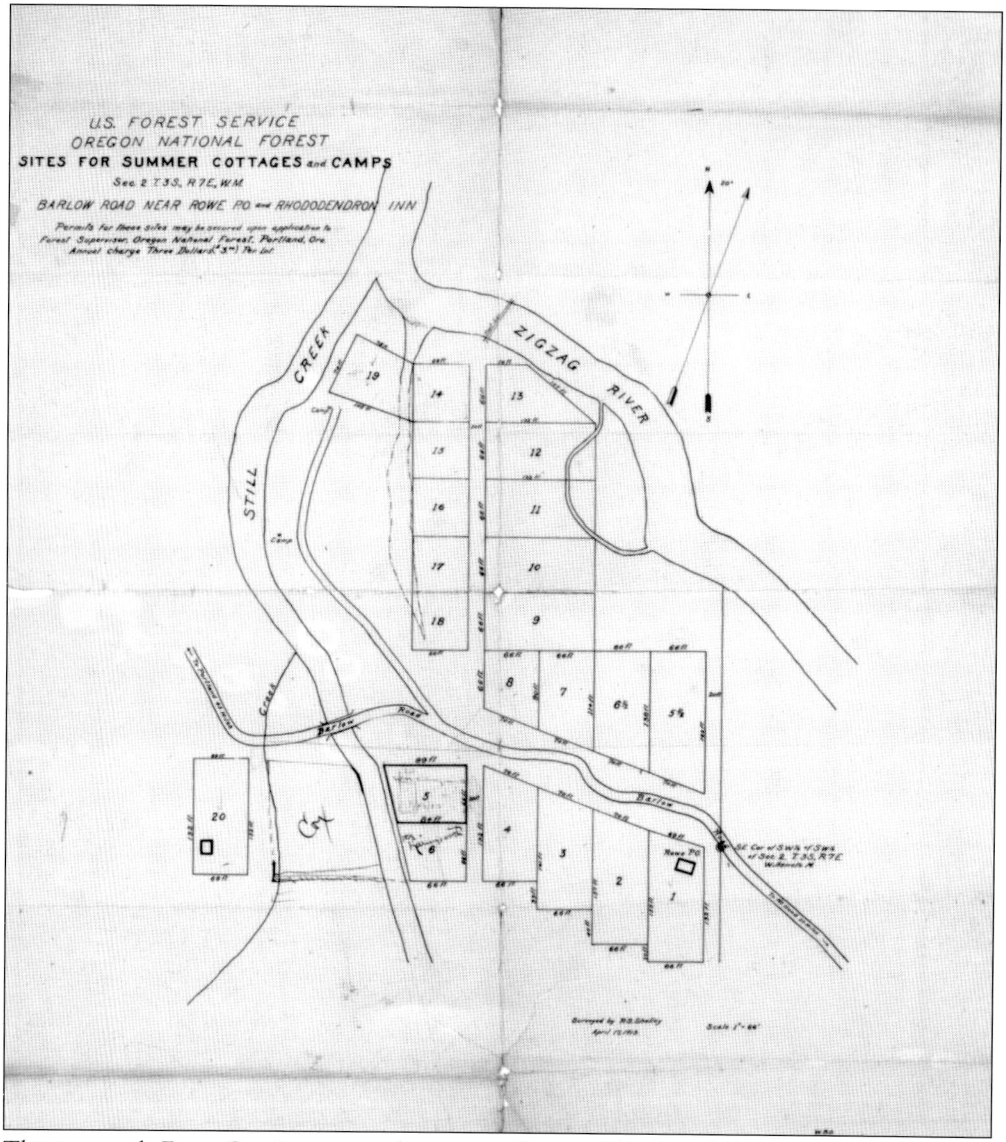

This is an early Forest Service summer home map. Surveyed by R.S. Shelley on April 17, 1913, the map shows the first platted areas for summer cottages and camps near the Rowe Post Office and the Rhododendron Inn. Permit applications for using the sites could be obtained from the Oregon National Forest for $3 per lot. It shows the Rowe Post Office located on Lot No. 1, close to where the Barlow Road Bridge crossed the Zigzag River. On the other side of the Zigzag River Bridge, but not identified on this map, was the location of Rhododendron Inn. (Courtesy of MHCC&M.)

A typical Forest Service summer home under construction in 1923 is shown here. Terms of the Forest Service permit stated that homes could be no larger than 1,200 square feet or 1,600 square feet if one and a half stories. Natural materials had to be used in the construction. If painted, earth-tone colors approved by the Forest Service had to be used. Each home was positioned to provide natural seclusion from neighboring homes. Most of the homes built on nearby private sites also followed these guidelines. (Courtesy of MHCC&M.)

A large majority of the homes in the Rhododendron area overlook a mountain stream. The Zigzag River, Still Creek, and Henry Creek all flow through the community. The primary natural vegetation consists of Douglas fir, western hemlock, western red cedar, and alder trees. The understory is dominated by the native pink flowering Pacific rhododendron, red huckleberry, Oregon grape, and salal. (Courtesy of MHCC&M.)

This Forest Service cabin was built in 1924 by John H. and Minnie Carson, who were the first Forest Service permit holders for this property. Originally named the Firs, it is currently owned by Jerry and Nancy King. As a career surveyor, Jerry understands the surveying mistake that occurred when Rhododendron was originally platted. In 1898, the US government contracted with Seth "Sledge" Tatum Jr. to subdivide a portion of Township 3 South, Range 7 East of the Willamette Meridian (Rhododendron). In 1903, Heinrich Haman received a patent for 160 acres that followed the surveyed boundaries. In 1911, Henry Rowe and the Rhododendron Mineral Springs Company recorded the Plat of Rhododendron, and in 1924, the Franzetti Addition was recorded, both following the 1898 boundaries. In 1932, a new survey revealed that Tatum's work in 1898 was "entirely fraudulent and fictitious!" In 1986, a US Forest Service survey established the true boundaries showing the areas of varying gaps between the two surveys, which included the narrative "No warranty, express or implied, is made as to the ownership in areas of overlap." (Courtesy of Jerry King.)

The Zigzag Auto Park Cabins were built by the Civilian Conservation Corps in 1933. In 1942, the six cabins were bought and managed by Marjorie and Lloyd Jenkins. They were located at the west end of Rhododendron along the Zigzag River approximately where Road 9 is now. The cabins featured stone fireplaces and neat, compact, attractive kitchens. Private picnic grounds were also provided. After being lost to floodwaters or torn down due to disrepair, only one cabin still exists. (Courtesy of Glenda Barbre.)

In 1965, the Forest Haven Motel was Rhododendron's newest and most modern lodging accommodation. It originally consisted of seven units, one being considerably larger than the others. They were generally rented by the ski crowd and accommodated two to four guests in each unit. Because the bigger unit could accommodate a family, it was in constant demand. The units are no longer a motel but serve as individual long-term rental cabins. They still exist and are located at the corner of Henry Creek Road and Highway 26. (Courtesy of Kathy Matter.)

The Zigzag Ranger Station compound dates to 1907, when the site was selected as the location for a ranger's headquarters. The name *Zigzag* was chosen by R.S. Shelley, who was a surveyor for the Forest Service. In a letter to acting forest supervisor R.B. Wilson, dated March 8, 1907, Shelley recommended the site and the name for the ranger's headquarters. The first Forest Service building at the Zigzag site was constructed in 1917. In 1929, this historic Roads and Trails Warehouse Building was constructed. (Courtesy of Zigzag Ranger Station.)

The Zigzag Ranger Station compound covers 125 acres. A large portion was built by the Civilian Conservation Corps between 1933 and 1942. Sites were selected for ranger stations at strategic locations within the national forest to support fire patrols and project crews working at remote forest sites. The Zigzag Ranger Station has served as a district headquarters since it was built. Because the station has unique historic value, the compound was listed in the National Register of Historic Places on April 8, 1986. (Courtesy of Zigzag Ranger Station.)

Six

Nature's Wrath

All east–west travel along Highway 26 came to an abrupt halt the afternoon of December 22, 1964, when the bridge crossing the Zigzag River was washed away by the tremendous force of the raging river's floodwaters. Referred to as "the 1964 Flood" or the "Christmas Flood," this historic 100-year event devastated roads, bridges, and many homes along the banks of creeks and rivers. The flood was regarded as one of the most destructive natural disasters ever recorded in the Pacific Northwest. (Courtesy of MHCC&M.)

The original pedestrian footbridge over the Zigzag River was built in the 1950s, after the Mount Hood Loop Highway bridge was demolished by the Oregon Department of Transportation and the newly constructed US Highway 26 became the new route into Rhododendron. The footbridge became affectionately referred to as "the Swinging Bridge." It was washed out in the 1964 Flood along with many cabins, homes, and bridges. But the cabin shown on the far bank of the Zigzag River, located on the peninsula, still stands today. (Courtesy of MHCC&M.)

Shown here is the Zigzag River on the south side of Rhododendron as it flows west. The buildings seen on the edge of the bank are the cabins and duplexes of the Snowline Motel. Most were torn down due unstable riverbanks and to damage from the flood. (Courtesy of Kathy Matter.)

This photograph shows a raging Still Creek flowing into the Zigzag River. Upstream from this confluence, both rivers had already washed away many homes and at least five bridges. The Zigzag River continued its uncontrolled destruction toward Zigzag, Oregon, where it joined the Sandy River. Between the towns of Rhododendron and Troutdale, over 155 homes were lost. Unfortunately, the flood claimed one life. After knowing his wife made it safely out, A. Harry Engols was unable to escape before the raging river claimed their home. His body was never recovered. (Courtesy of MHCC&M.)

With roads and bridges washed away, Joie Smith rigged up a primitive bosun's chair across the Zigzag River. Since the river was impossible to cross, a bow and arrow were used to shoot string to people on the opposite bank, allowing them to draw cable to help rig the chair. After the chair was secured, Joie was able to send food, supplies, hay for livestock, and even people back and forth until the roads reopened. In this photograph, Juanita Anliker is riding the rope seat across the Zigzag River. (Courtesy of Kathy Matter.)

Rebuilding roads and bridges began almost immediately after the flood. The Army Corps of Engineers showed up en masse, as did emergency crews from Clackamas County and the state. The priority was to get at least some of the bridges rebuilt so transportation could begin delivery of the necessary rebuilding supplies. (Courtesy of MHCC&M.)

After the flood, the top priority was bridge construction. Access to Rhododendron and Government Camp from Portland, as well as from Hood River and Bend, was completely cut off. The White River Bridge on Highway 35 was washed away, and the roads and bridges along Highway 26 into Bend were either washed out or threatened. Here, construction workers are hard at work reconstructing a bridge over the Zigzag River. (Courtesy of MHCC&M.)

The Hartness cabin (in the trees) was built by George and Helen Hartness in 1920. Located at the south end of the original Road 20 bridge over the Zigzag River (foreground), it was one of the first vacation homes built and was much larger than many of the summer cabins. In 1919, George qualified to join the Mazamas, a mountaineering club, by climbing Mount Rainier. He then went on to climb Mount Hood 22 times. The Hartnesses enjoyed coming to their mountain house from Portland to relax in front of the fireplace. But in 1964, this house, the bridge, and most of the road fell victim to the Christmas Flood. (Both, courtesy of Alice Hartness Reichle.)

In late December 1964, after weeks of frigid temperatures, frozen ground, and heavy snowfall, a tropical weather system called a "Pineapple Express" brought warm rain and even warmer chinook winds to the Pacific Northwest. Temperatures rose 30 to 40 degrees within a few hours. On the night of December 21 and throughout the day of December 22, the warm rains quickly melted the glacial snow, but with the ground still frozen, the water could not be absorbed. Massive amounts of melted snow flooded into all the mountain rivers leading to the Sandy River Basin. As the raging torrents of the Zigzag River, Still Creek, and Henry Creek took out trees and riverbanks, the accumulated debris caused towering log jams at numerous bridges. With the debris load too much to bear, the bridges collapsed, sending torrents of water and more debris down river, indiscriminately destroying many homes and vacation cabins. The Hartness cabin, seen here on the right, hanging over the edge, was located on the hill above the washed-out Road 20 Zigzag River Bridge. (Courtesy of Alice Hartness Reichle.)

After the flood, access into Rhododendron was cut off for many who lived on the peninsula bounded by the Zigzag River on one side and Still Creek on the other. All road bridges, as well as the pedestrian bridge across the Zigzag River, were gone. In order to cross the river to obtain some necessary supplies still available from the Rhododendron store, Jack O'Brien constructed this makeshift footbridge. (Courtesy of the O'Brien family.)

One of the original cabins built in Rhododendron was Wilbur and Evelyn Reid's Alderbrook Lodge. The floodwaters of the Zigzag River rose over 15 feet in this area, brushing under the porch of this summer home. An unidentified member of the Reid family stands vigil watching the floodwaters rush by. (Courtesy of Matt Reid.)

Alderbrook Lodge narrowly escaped the rushing Zigzag River floodwaters. In this photograph, the corner of the home was saved by Joie Smith, a relative of the Reid family, who stabilized and moved dirt to minimize further erosion. During the repair phase of the flood cleanup, the US Army Corps of Engineers bulldozed the river channels and placed riprap along the river edges in an effort to tame the seasonally raging river. (Courtesy of Matt Reid.)

Here are Walt and Pat Aeppli at their home in Rhododendron. Growing up in Zurich, Switzerland, Walt served in the Swiss Army during World War II and was trained as an engineer. He moved to the United States in 1948 and quickly met friends with European backgrounds and formed the group Edelweiss Irregulars. On weekends, they would sing and play the accordion at Timberline Lodge. With his love for the mountain and his engineering background, Walt was quickly hired at Timberline as the chief engineer, working until his retirement in 1987. (Courtesy of Shelby Aeppli Imholt.)

In 1961, the Aeppli family posed for this photograph. Pat met Walt while working at Timberline Lodge during the summer of 1951. They were married in March 1952. Their first daughter, Christine Susi, was born in December 1952. Their second daughter, Shelby Ann, was born in January 1956. After marriage and two girls, Pat worked as the site manager at the Homestead Girl Scout Camp and as a clerk at the Rhododendron Post Office. (Courtesy of Shelby Aeppli Imholt.)

Located along Still Creek, the Aepplis' home was large and comfortable. Christie and Shelby Aeppli went to school as usual on the morning of December 22 but were sent home early because of the storm. The girls were met by Pat and Walt where the bus had to stop due to a washed-out bridge. The family walked to the house, but the raging creek was already very close. They gathered up the dog, cat, Christmas presents, and what clothes they could carry. By that evening, the entire house was swept away by the 1964 Christmas Flood. (Courtesy of Shelby Aeppli Imholt.)

This photograph of Pat Aeppli with her daughters, Christie (center) and Shelby (right), was found by a neighbor along the banks of Still Creek after the 1964 Christmas Flood. The Aeppli family lost their entire house and belongings to the flood. Of all of her belongings, Christie was most saddened with the loss of her favorite doll, dressed as a bride. A few weeks after the flood, while inspecting the creek, a worker with Portland General Electric (PGE) found a doll caked with mud but otherwise in good shape. He took it home to his own little girl, who cleaned it up. Later, the PGE worker met Walt Aeppli at Timberline, and as they discussed the flood, Walt shared his story with the man. The worker went home and told his family about the Aeppli family. As a gesture of kindness, his daughter wanted him to give the doll he found to Christie, which he did. Christie and Shelby could not believe the worker had found Christie's favorite doll. (Courtesy of Shelby Aeppli Imholt.)

Seven

But Wait . . . There's More

Fire has always been a threat in the Mount Hood National Forest. Lookouts were placed on the highest hills and manned 24/7 during fire seasons. Zigzag Mountain rises to the north of Rhododendron. Shown here is the Zigzag Mountain Lookout in the Mount Hood National Forest. It was built in 1932 and deactivated in 1964. Shortly after deactivation, the lookout was purposely destroyed by the Forest Service in a controlled burn. (Courtesy of MHCC&M.)

In 1916, the Multnomah Chapter of Daughters of the American Revolution (DAR) placed this bronze marker in Rhododendron commemorating the Oregon Trail. At the dedication ceremony were six descendants of Sam Barlow, including his granddaughters, great-granddaughters, and even a great-great-granddaughter. The marker is located along US Highway 26 and Arlie Mitchell Road and is identified as an 1845 Oregon Trail Historical Site. (Both, authors' collection.)

The Rhododendron Community Planning Organization maintains the Rhododendron Garden surrounding the DAR memorial. It is located along Highway 26 and can be seen as travelers enter Rhododendron from the west. Pictured here from left to right are Merv Novinger, Dan Holm, an unidentified young man, and Nancy Dougherty. (Courtesy of Nancy Dougherty.)

This Mount Hood National Forest marker is on the corner of East Lolo Pass Road and US Highway 26 across from the Zigzag Ranger Station. Arlie Mitchell carved the Mount Hood rock image on the marker. He and George Pinner, who was partially blind at the time, built the stone marker, which still stands today. (Courtesy of Rebecca Copley.)

Richard "Dick" Dopp graduated in 1964 from the University of Wisconsin with a degree in civil engineering. He was hired by Clackamas County, and his first project was designing a pedestrian bridge to replace the original footbridge that had washed away in the 1964 Flood. Dopp recalls that he was not quite sure what he was doing, as he had never designed a cable suspension bridge before. Upon completion, Dopp was amazed that his engineering calculations actually worked. (Courtesy of Richard Dopp.)

The Rhododendron Footbridge is affectionately known to some local folks as "the Swinging Bridge." It was rebuilt by Clackamas County in 2017 after 52 years of wear and tear. During the rebuilding process, Clackamas County took great effort to retain the original inscription of "DICK DOPP '65" that is bead welded on the bridge's threshold. (Authors' collection.)

The rebuilt Rhododendron Footbridge was dedicated in September 2017. During the dedication ceremony, from left to right, Clackamas County commissioners Jim Bernard, Ken Humberston, and Paul Savas read a proclamation stating that the Clackamas County Board of Commissioners dedicated the Rhododendron Footbridge over the Zigzag River to the residents of the Mount Hood Territory, the Hoodland area, and the Rhododendron community. (Authors' collection.)

On January 26, 2020, the Rhododendron Post Office celebrated its centennial. A well-attended celebration was held at the Still Creek Inn (originally the Alpine Hut) with numerous guest speakers expounding about the rich history of Rhododendron. In honor of that occasion, Renee Lamoreaux-Robinson designed a special cancellation stamp that was used by the Rhododendron Post Office, to the thrill of philatelists and memorabilia collectors. (Courtesy of Renee Lamoreaux-Robinson.)

As Rhododendron celebrates its centennial, the community is at a crossroad. The future of Rhododendron has yet to be written, but if past history is any reflection on the resilience and character of the people, places, and events that helped shape the community, then the future of Rhododendron looks bright. (Courtesy of Laurie Crabb and the Rhododendron Community Planning Organization.)

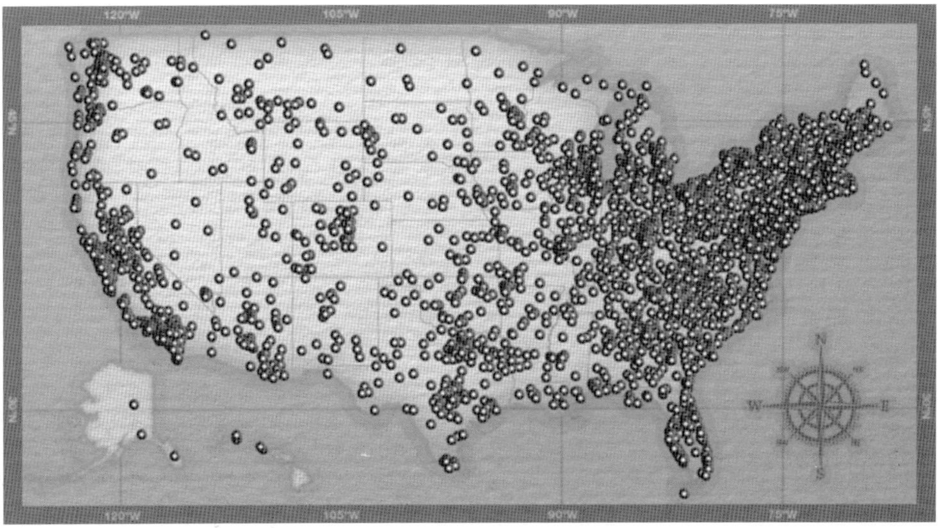